Religious Language
Philosophy of Religion Coursebook

Stephen Loxton

Published by Inducit Learning Ltd,

Mid Somerset House, Southover, Wells BA5 1UH, United Kingdom

www.pushmepress.com

First published in 2013

ISBN: 978-1-909618-46-6

Contents

Introduction

The topic of religious language has engaged some of the most original thinkers in the tradition. Our task in this book is to take a look at the key thinkers and aim to understand them and the way their arguments impinge on each other in relation to the core issues.

Philosophy of Religion has a two-fold character. Some philosophers of religion use philosophical argument and technique to develop a rationale for faith; others are primarily concerned with the examination and analysis of religious beliefs and concepts. These two ways can, of course, be combined. Philosophers of religion are interested in what **RELIGIOUS BELIEFS** mean, in the issue of whether religious beliefs are true and of whether and how religious beliefs are meaningful. A philosopher of religion might be interested in how religious beliefs fit in with other beliefs, in how religious knowledge is like – or unlike – the knowledge we have (or think we have) in history, biology or mathematics. Philosophy of religion is thus likely to focus on the **NATURE, PURPOSE, MEANING** and **VALUE** of religious language.

With regard to the problem of religious language, a common question is that of how or by what means religious language is significant. This means that questions focus on the meaning of language that expresses religious faith, belief, or truth. The key question is then, given that we might claim to know how language usually works, in what legitimate sense is religious language **TRUE**? This can be expressed as the question as to whether religious language is **COGNITIVELY SIGNIFICANT**? Can such language express **KNOWABLE TRUTHS**, truths that are genuinely a matter of justified knowledge?

The OCR specification (G581) gives some very clear pointers to what is to be studied: candidates have to show that they know and understand the use and purpose of religious language; this means knowing how, within specific religious or faith traditions the distinctive language of that tradition is deployed. We will say more on this in a moment.

Next there are some clear areas of study to examine:

- The "via negativa" - or the Apophatic way.

- The verification and falsification principles.

- Different views on the meaningfulness of religious language.

- The uses of symbol, analogy and myth to express human understanding of God.

- The views of the Vienna Circle, A. J. Ayer, Anthony Flew, Ludwig Wittgenstein and Paul Tillich on religious language.

The expectation is that students prepare so that they can "discuss these areas critically and their strengths and weaknesses"; an ongoing aim through this book is to cultivate via critical exposition the ability to assess critically the material we are examining. To help this, key terms and self-assessment questions appear at the end of each chapter, and the last two self-assessment questions each time are based on the question style of OCR's A2 paper.

Before we get into the main business of the topics we have to review let's pick up on the point mentioned earlier, that a basic aspect of the religious language topic is to **KNOW** and **UNDERSTAND** the use and purpose of religious language.

THE USE AND PURPOSE OF RELIGIOUS LANGUAGE

Consider the following example:

If I am walking along the street where I live and someone driving by stops and asks me the way to the local Church, and I give her directions so she can find it, I have used a word, a noun, "Church", a part of common speech in English. It denotes a religious building within the Christian religion. Have I, in using this word, been using some "religious language"? In a general sense, I have.

In a similar way if I was asked directions to the local football stadium by a visiting fan, and I explained how she could get there, would I be using the "language of football"? Again, in a general sense I would be.

However, suppose I enter a Church, cross myself before the altar, kneel and begin to recite "Our Father, Hallowed be thy name, Thy kingdom come, forgive us our sins as we forgive those who have sinned against us …" Have I used religious language? Have I used religious language in a way that is different from giving directions to the Church?

Or suppose I go the football stadium, find my friends who are all there to support the home team, and join in with them with the gestures, songs and chants that express our support for the team, and engage in discussion over who is playing and whether 4-4-2 will really be effective against today's opposition. Have I been using "the language of football"? Have I been using it in a different way from the way I used it when giving someone directions to the stadium?

In both cases, going into the Church and praying, and going to the football ground to actively support my team, my language-use is surely qualitatively different from my mode of language-use when giving

directions. In the street and giving directions my usage is **FUNCTIONAL,**
OPERATIONAL, and **UNCOMMITTED.** In the Church at prayer and in
the stadium supporting my team my language signals **COMMITMENT,**
ENGAGEMENT and **PARTICIPATION** in the faith perspective of my
Church and my football team.

From this we can see that when we discuss "religious language" it is
important to keep in mind that what we are examining will be the
language of religious faith, commitment and engagement. This would
include the language of prayer, devotion, meditation, creeds, hymns,
theological doctrine, scriptural writing, and over and above what will
follow in this book, having plenty of examples of such language to hand
to use to illustrate what else you might want to argue is a good idea.

Note too that in the examples what went on was not just spoken
language: a part of a faith commitment is the language of gesture; faith
is expressed through actions as well as through words - and this appears
to be the case whether you observe what goes in a Church or at a
football match.

Apophatic Thought and Analogy

In the first part of this chapter we will examine the apophatic approach to theological language, and then we will consider Aquinas' doctrine of analogy.

THE APOPHATIC WAY

The term "apophatic" means a method of affirming something by systematic denial. Many religious thinkers suggest that if God is Holy and eternal, and humans are finite and imperfect, then the only way to express what "God" means or what faith in God entails is by saying what he is not. To "affirm via negation" is to operate apophatically and the apophatic tradition or the via negativa is a pervasive theme in this whole topic.

The writer Pseudo Dionysius the Aeropagite, thought to have been active around 500CE, develops a sense of contrast between cataphatic theology, and apophatic theology, and then he advocates a third approach known as the **VIA EMINENTIAE** (the way of eminence).

What was meant by these three terms?

Within the orthodox traditions of Christianity the distinctions here are maintained as of great importance. **CATAPHATIC THEOLOGY** involves using normal terms like "light", "goodness", "justice" or "love" - terms that have resonance within usual human discourse, to suggest something of the nature and character of God. But since God is experienced as transcendent, other, and as Holy, the literal application of these terms does not serve the task of expressing what is encountered in faith.

Christians in the Russian Orthodox traditions are clear about the issues here:

> "In our understanding of God we often rely upon cataphatic notions since these are easier and more accessible to the mind. But cataphatic knowledge has its limits. The way of negation corresponds to the spiritual ascent into the Divine abyss where words fall silent, where reason fades, where all human knowledge and comprehension cease, where God is."

The "way of negation" here is the "via negativa" or apophatic way, and on this it is said:

> "When discussing the names of God, we inevitably conclude that not one of them can give us a complete idea of who He is. To speak of the attributes of God is to discover that their sum total is not God. God transcends any name. If we call Him being, He transcends being, He is supra-being. If we ascribe to Him righteousness and justice, in His love He transcends all justice. If we call Him love, He is much more than human love: He is supra-love. God transcends all attributes that we are capable of ascribing to Him, be it omniscience, omnipresence or immutability. Ultimately we arrive at the conclusion that we can say nothing about God affirmatively: all discussion about Him remains incomplete, partial and limited. Finally we come to realize that we cannot say what God is, but rather what He is not. This manner of speaking about God has received the name of apophatic (negative) theology, as opposed to cataphatic (affirmative) theology."

In similar manner, Pseudo-Dionysius writes that God, "is not soul, not intellect … not greatness, not smallness … not moved, not at rest, not powerful, not power … not living, not life … not one, not unity, not divinity, not goodness … not something among what is, not something among what is not." (1980 p. 221-222)

The "via eminentiae" for Pseudo Dionysius and for Russian Orthodoxy today is the approach taken in and through faith that moves beyond trying to predicate qualities of God and on to the state of devotion or worship.

> *"It is not by speculative knowledge but in the depths of prayerful silence that the soul can encounter God, Who is 'beyond everything' and Who reveals Himself to her as in-comprehensible, in-accessible, in-visible, yet at the same time as living and close to her - as God the Person."*

(The material here is quoted from the website of the Russian Orthodox Church in the UK).

The apophatic approach is also associated with the mystic St John of the Cross (1542- 1591) and to the view that it is through a certain pattern of reflection and experience that a mystical contemplation of or union with the ineffable divine is possible. But such experience or insight is distinct and irreducible, and so it cannot be adequately expressed in human terms. Again, what we can follow is the apophatic approach of affirming through **NEGATION**; God is **NOT** finite, **NOT** evil, **NOT** partial, **NOT** limited, **NOT** impure, and so on. A key point to convey is that it is not possible for man to say what God is in any sense that is definitive.

The Jewish theologian Moses Maimonides (1136-1204) is another thinker in the tradition of apophatic thought.

The writer of the Psalms gives us the core sense of the points he wants to make about talk of God;

"For God alone my soul waits in silence." (Psalm 62:1)

And we can cite this passage from Isaiah:

"Truly, you are a God who hides himself." (Isaiah 45.13))

Maimonides' view was that any statement declaring a specific quality or attribute of God could not but be a limitation of what God is. God was something we might encounter, but God was not, he thought, something we could express.

In The Guide for the Perplexed Maimonides gives an example to show the "impropriety" of "ascribing to God any positive attributes" and the "propriety of forming as many negative attributes as possible":

"A person may know for certain that a 'ship' is in existence, but he may not know to what object that name is applied, whether to a substance or to an accident; a second person then learns that a ship is not an accident; a third person that it is not a mineral; a fourth that it is not a plant growing in the earth; a fifth that it is not a body whose parts are joined together by nature; a sixth, that not a flat object like boards or doors; a seventh, that is not a sphere; an eighth, that it is not pointed; a ninth, that it is not round shaped; not equilateral; a tenth, that it is not solid. It is clear that this tenth person has almost arrived at the correct notion of a 'ship' by the foregoing negative attributes... In the same manner you will come nearer to the knowledge and comprehension of God by the negative attributes

... I do not merely declare that he who affirms attributes of God has not sufficient knowledge concerning the Creator ... but I say that he unconsciously loses his belief in God ... " (The Guide for the Perplexed LX p. 169)

How did Maimonides come to this view?

- He was steeped in the Jewish tradition of monotheism and regarded God as sovereign.

- He was influenced by Aristotelian views of causation to see that God should be regarded as the prior cause of all and thus outside the pattern of cause and effect.

- Thus God should be seen as outside of and prior to time and space.

- All this implies - as in the wisdom tradition in Judaism - that God is unique, holy and pure.

This then means that any expression of description of God that is anthropocentric must not be understood literally but metaphorically. This includes Biblical accounts such as Moses' encounter with God through a burning bush or receiving the Ten Commandments from God on Mount Sinai. (Exodus 3 & 20). Maimonides is thus arguing for a metaphorical approach to biblical interpretation, for a non-literal reading of scripture.

Maimonides is stressing that human language is used to distinguish, to define, to explain - and it does this well in respect of things within the domain of finite experience which can be dismantled and explained linguistically. But "God" would not be "God" if He were available to be spoken of in this way.

Problems for Maimonides and for Apophatic Thought

A commonly observed problem with Maimonides's example of the ship is as follows. Suppose someone has grasped all of the negative attributes that are mentioned; are they then in possession of the correct notion of a ship? It can be argued that a person is just as close to an understanding something like a box or a cupboard.

A common criticism made in various ways is that religious language is contradictory, or incoherent, or meaningless. But on the other hand the tradition of apophatic thought suggests that apparently contradictory language-use is legitimate when it is employed to indicate a sense of what lies beyond what can be expressed in normal human concepts. There is a tension here.

So the philosopher Bernard Williams (1929-2003) suggests that as a matter of fact a key feature of theological language is that it has "a sort of inherent and necessary incomprehensibility," (Williams in Flew and MacIntyre, 1955:187)

Williams is, like Maimonides, clear that this is because such language tries to express a relation between the natural and the supernatural. And Williams thinks the problem can be pressed. If we use human terms in talking of God we still have the problem of understanding what we mean:

> "Religious language requires merely an extrapolation from the human context, is not to solve the problem, but to pose it again. For the extrapolation is to infinity, and in even trying to give a sense to this we encounter the incomprehensibility." (1955:204)

Williams does not think an apophatic solution is helpful. He thinks that theological insight is claimed for something that by definition cannot be understood. This results in the person of faith being asked to believe on trust something they cannot know to be true, or to be distinct from something that might be false (1955:208ff).

Defenders of the apophatic approach argue that the negation or contradiction of regular concepts is consistent with a type of theological insight which uses paradoxical language to express God's nature. If "God" is defined as Anselm suggests as "something greater (more perfect) than it is possible to think" (Proslogion 15) then it is logically consistent to say that "God" is beyond literal description, so that all apparently affirmative descriptive terms must be negated. On this reasoning, a large problem exists for theological and religious language if it is treated as the language of description; conversely, the more the "apophatic" use of language is promoted, the more the transcendence of "God" or "the ultimate" will be signalled.

This leads to the view that the paradoxical character of apophatic language is important as it protects the sanctity and transcendence of God from literalism, anthropomorphism, and other reductions.

The philosopher John Wisdom (1904-1993) makes some relevant remarks on this issue. Commenting on the role of paradoxes in general he says that:

> "I wish to represent them as... symptoms of linguistic penetration." (Wisdom 1953:41)

Wisdom continues to argue that there is philosophical usefulness about paradoxes, the key point being that:

> "Their philosophical usefulness depends upon their

paradoxicalness and thus upon their falsehood. They are false
because they are needed where ordinary language
fails." (1953:50)

Further problems for the via negativa

It is easy to see what the via negativa is trying to do; in contrast with the via positiva of the cataphatic way, it tries to protect the status and distinctiveness of the concept of God. The ultimate subject of religious experience is inexpressible; the infinite is not and cannot be expressed as that which is finite.

But there is still a logical problem. We can still ask, "What is it that is expressed via the silence of the apophatic way?"

If we say "God is in inexpressible" we are still expressing something about "God". We mean that "God" is inexpressible, so we are saying something about "God", we are giving a description of some kind. But the meaning of the description is that it isn't one - nothing is described. This can be seen as a paradox - or as a contradiction.

Further, it is often argued that faith in "God" and experience of "God" are what make the difference to one's life. The idea is that through faith commitment and via religious experience 'God' enters into some form of relationship with humanity, and if such experience is possible, it must be distinguishable. We must be able to notice it as distinct from other experiences and other forms of commitment. If this is so then it must a form of experience of or commitment to a "something" that we can in some way express.

Here we hit on perhaps the key role of religious language, the language that is employed to point to a mode of experience and to a pattern of life which is the religious response to reality.

Perhaps one key to understanding the nature and role of religious language is to see that the absolute, ultimate or Holy, is, in religious traditions ancient and modern, commonly seen to be transcending that which is found in and though religious experience.

Ninian Smart (1927-2001) makes the point well:

> "Concepts apply to God's manifested activity... not to his unmanifested essence... It is not just that God transcends the world: he transcends himself as known to us." (1970:50)

This point is a valuable corrective to the view of some in the apophatic strand of thought who want to argue that God is wholly other:

> "The rigid doctrine of the wholly other would seem... to mean that no predicate which can truly be predicated of anything in the world can be predicated truly of God." (1970:63)

The problem with this is as follows:

> "The concept of the religious ultimate in practice is the concept of something which, though it may lie beyond its manifestations, nevertheless manifests itself in the world here and there and somehow. But if the rigid doctrine of the wholly other were correct, no predicate by which we describe a manifestation of the religious ultimate could be truly predicated of the religious ultimate. We could not, for example, use the term 'Holy' of God. By a paradox there would no resemblance between God and his manifestations." (1970:63-64)

Smart hints at an approach to religious language where myth, metaphor and symbol all have a significant role to play - matters we look at in detail in due course.

AQUINAS AND THE DOCTRINE OF ANALOGY

Aquinas (1224-1274) makes a very significant contribution to the issues raised by religious language - in particular he contributes a key idea through his doctrine of analogy.

According to Aquinas "whatever is said of God and creatures" is said "in an analogous sense." (Summa Theologica, 1, 13, 5).

Aquinas' teaching on analogy involves an important distinction we need to keep in mind:

Analogy of Proportion

This is when we use a word to refer to an attribute of a thing but to indicate in due proportion the degree of reality that the thing in question has. Aquinas has in mind the common observation from general experience which shows that language is often used in an analogical way to express similarities between things that enjoy rather different modes of being.

A common example is the use of the term faithfulness in respect of a dog and a friend. Aquinas would see this as a case of analogy "downwards", from the level of humanity to the realm of (other) animals. It seems obvious that if we speak of a friend and of our dog as being faithful, we are not using the term in the same sense in relation to both - our use is not univocal. Our dog isn't faithful in the same way as our friend.

However, it certainly isn't the case that we are using the term "faithful" in an equivocal manner, with a quite different sense or meaning in relation to each referent.

What we are doing is to use the term in an analogical fashion: there is a similarity between the attitudes of the dog and of our friend such that the term is appropriate in relation to both.

However, we are aware of the difference between the two, so that there can be no question of putting the two on the same level via the use of the term. Our friend possesses, shall we say, a far more definite sense of responsibility, consciousness and moral intent. It is his faithfulness that determines the idea of faithfulness we see reflected in the relationship we have with our dog. In the attitude of the dog we see something which corresponds in relative terms to the attitude we fully understand at the interpersonal level. Nevertheless, the analogy permits the claim that it is true that the dog is faithful; that the claim is understood to convey meaning and knowledge concerning experience.

Analogy of Attribution

The workings of analogy from humanity to animals above is complimented by its use in talk of God, in which use, as Aquinas understands it, it is the divine not the human aspect that determines the meaning of the predicate, quality or relation. Thus human wisdom, goodness, benevolence, or grace derives from the nature and will of the divine. This is a truth known in and through the experience of faith. It means that the information or knowledge that is conveyed via analogy comes through a negation of the common human meaning of the term, with the various constraints that surround it in the finite domain of its regular usage, so that the pure and intrinsic meaning can be made clear.

Aquinas thinks that we see that the attributes we sometimes show - of sickness on the one hand, or of devotion on the other, are attributes analogically expressed of disease in the first case, and of God's devotion, in the other.

Aquinas considers that unequivocal language use is inappropriate for language about God, and that and equivocal use is of no value in the communication of meaning. Analogical use, Aquinas thinks, works well, and largely this is because his prior faith perspective, that God is creator and so source or explanation for everything, means there is an **ANALOGIA ENTIS**, an analogy of being, between God and his creation. In this way analogy of attribution can work proportionally.

Some problems with analogy

1. One problem seen with analogy is that if an analogy works it is usually because there is a shared understanding between the two areas of experience. If I suggest that John has "played with a straight bat" in making a deal with me to buy a house, the analogy between a correct technique in cricket and fairness in making a deal works if we who use it share understanding about cricket and deals on houses. But we might, on Kantian grounds, argue that we don't "know" God; "God" is defined as being beyond the confines of the space-time phenomenal world within which we can know things, with Kant claiming that he denies "knowledge" (of God) to "make room for faith" (in God). (Kant 1929 p. 29). The implication here is that we can't use language analogically and know that it works proportionally on both sides. This is a similar problem to the point raised by Williams against apophatic thought, discussed earlier.

2. A similar objection could arise from New Testament thought. Paul writes as follows to the Corinthians: "For now we see through a glass darkly, but then face to face; now I know in part; but then shall I know even as also I am known." (1 Corinthians 13.12) This view implies that no sense that is clear or certain could be possible in the finite domain in relation to the supposed object of faith - but the life of faith, by default, entails hope as to a future state when resolution would occur.

3. The idea of God as Creator as expressed by Aquinas, involves the view that all that is in the creature must first of all and essentially be possessed by the creator. This is said to mean that via the analogia entis there can be legitimate analogical language about God. This can be seen to entail a logically challenging dilemma.

4. Suppose I adapt Aquinas' view to the statement that "All that is in the creature must first of all and essentially be possessed by the creator". Is this meant to be a literal or an analogical proposition? If Aquinas means that "All that is in the creature must first of all and essentially be possessed by the creator" is literally true, then not all language about God is analogical, and Aquinas contradicts his own theory. If however Aquinas argues that "All that is in the creature must first of all and essentially be possessed by the creator" is analogical, then in effect he is explaining analogies with analogy, and that is a circular argument.

SELF-ASSESSMENT QUESTIONS

1. Define and illustrate the apophatic approach to religious/theological language.

2. Explain and illustrate the method implied by the via negativa.

3. Set out and explain Maimonides' argument using his example of the ship.

4. Make clear notes of the problems and criticisms raised against the role of paradox in the apophatic approach.

5. Explain and illustrate using your own examples the differences in language use between univocal, equivocal and analogical usage.

6. Explain and illustrate Aquinas' idea of analogy of attribution.

7. Explain and illustrate Aquinas' idea of analogy of proportion.

8. Make clear notes of the problems raised against the use of analogy to justify religious/theological language.

And two A2-style questions:

9. "The only way in which meaningful statements can be made about God is the via negativa." Discuss.

10. To what extent is the doctrine of analogy able to counter the charge that religious language is meaningless because it is non-verifiable?

KEY TERMS

Cataphatic/Apophatic - the Via Negativa/Via eminentiae - Mysticism - Paradox - Univocal Language - Equivocal Language - Analogical Language - Analogy of Attribution - Analogy of Proportion

FURTHER READING

Smart (1970) has a valuable discussion of apophatic thought and Davies (1992) is very helpful on Aquinas and Analogy.

Verification and Falsification

During the twentieth century a good deal of debate over religious language centred around two principles: the principle of verification and the principle of falsification.

Both provide specific challenges to the view that religious language could be a legitimate vehicle for meaning and knowledge.

We now come to a clear overlap between four items listed in the exam specification: the principle of verification, Ludwig Wittgenstein, the Vienna Circle and A.J. Ayer.

The principle of verification has its origin in the discussions of the "Vienna Circle". This was the name adopted by a group of thinkers - mathematicians, philosophers, scientists and political theorists all working at the University of Vienna - the **"LOGICAL POSITIVISTS"** as they also became known, who met from 1922 to 1936. Their aim was to review philosophical problems and re-orientate philosophy tightly to the methods and values of mathematics and natural science. The British philosopher A.J. Ayer (1910-1989) visited the Vienna Circle and his subsequent work popularised their views. The term "logical positivism" came to be used for the ideas of the Vienna Circle and Ayer since they claimed that meaningful language was diagnosed by either logical or positivistic means, where "positivism" here is the continental term for the scientific method.

Key figures in the Vienna Circle included R. Carnap, M. Schlick, O. Neurath, and F. Waismann. They were influenced by Ludwig Wittgenstein (1889-1951), particularly by his book Tractatus Logico-Philosophicus

(1921). Wittgenstein's ideas will be considered in a later chapter. Here we can note that during the 1920s members of the Vienna Circle sought to draw Wittgenstein into their group. He decided after a few meetings that they were misunderstanding him and refused to continue discussions with them.

The Key Ideas of the Vienna Circle

The philosophers in the Vienna Circle did not think that philosophy had to do with describing and explaining the natural world - that was the task of the various sciences. It was the task of philosophy to provide clarification and analysis of method and argument.

Thus science was a "first order" activity because it dealt with the world: philosophy was a "second order" activity because it cultivated methods to analyse, check and verify statements.

The logical positivists believed that their approach could generate clear methodological principles to provide objective criteria for knowledge and belief. The Vienna Circle had a common interest with the tradition of analytical and empirical philosophy in Britain. As mentioned, A.J. Ayer, having visited Vienna and spent time with "Circle", returned to Oxford and wrote the book, Language, Truth and Logic (1936) that did most to promote the views of the group.

Ayer made explicit the principle of verification as the device to carry out the task of establishing meaning. Ayer expressed the view shared by the other logical positivists that truths could be expressed in, and only in, propositional form.

A proposition was an assertion of truth-expressing statement or sentence.

For example, "Today is the 15th of October" and "A spinster is an unmarried woman" are two "propositional" statements. Various empirical checks on calendars, newspapers and so on will establish whether or not today is the 15th of October, and we will then know whether the proposition "Today is the 15th of October" is, in fact, true or false. With the proposition "A spinster is an unmarried woman", a check on reference works and dictionaries will show that the proposition is a linguistic definition and so true by definition within the language use of English.

Ayer and the logical positivists thus took the view that for assertions or propositions to be significant, for them to have meaning, we must be able to determine their **COGNITIVE** status, that is, it must be possible for us to verify and so know how they might be shown to be true or false.

Accordingly, Ayer maintained that genuine propositions fell into one or the other of two basic classes: significant propositions must be either "the a priori propositions of logic and pure mathematics", or propositions "concerning empirical matters of fact." (1970:31)

Ayer terms the propositions that came into the first category "analytic" and those that fell into the second group "synthetic". His definition of the two types is as follows:

> "A proposition is analytic when its validity depends solely upon
> the definitions of the symbols it contains, and synthetic when its
> validity is determined by the facts of experience." (1970:78)

Ayer explains that:

> "The a priori propositions of logic and pure mathematics" are

*"necessary and certain only because they are analytic. That is ...
that the reason why these propositions cannot be confuted in
experience is that they do not make any assertion about the
empirical world, but simply record our determination to use
symbols in a certain fashion." (1970:31)*

Ayer considers that such propositions will exhibit literal significance.

In contrast, synthetic propositions concerning empirical matters of fact
are "hypotheses, which can be probable but never certain."

Such propositions have "factual significance"; Ayer argues that factual
significance can only come from the positivist method of observation and
verification:

*"A sentence is factually significant to a given person, if, and only
if, he knows how to verify the proposition which it purports to
express - that is, if he knows what observations would lead him,
under certain conditions, to accept the proposition as being true,
or refute it as being false." (1970:35)*

Ayer is also clear on some important differences in the types of
verification that are possible. He distinguishes between **PRACTICAL
VERIFIABILITY** and **VERIFIABILITY IN PRINCIPLE**. (1970:36) He
also distinguishes between strong and weak senses of the term
"verifiable" (1970:37)

By "practical verifiability" he means, in the case of propositions
concerning factual significance, those propositions that we could, in fact,
verify "if we took enough trouble". For example, suppose I say "There
about 60 million people living in the UK". Obviously to verify this factual
proposition I would have to go to some trouble, to check the latest

census data, the national birth and death rates, the data on immigration and emigration, and eventually I could get a verified but still probable answer.

By "verifiability in principle", Ayer means what we have with a significant factual proposition (such as "there is intelligent life elsewhere in the Universe") but lack the means to actually verify it. We lack the means "to make the relevant observations", is Ayer's way of putting it.

Ayer likes this distinction because it allows him to explain that by his criteria, a metaphysical statement such as "the Absolute enters into, but is itself incapable of, evolution and progress," cannot be "even in principle, verifiable." By the same token theological statements, such as God is infinitely wise and just, will not, even in principle, be verifiable.

The strong sense of verification comes with the view that a proposition is verified, "if, and only if, its truth could be conclusively established in experience." (1970:37)

In contrast, a proposition is verified in the weak sense "if it is possible for experience to render it probable."

Ayer thinks that the view that only the "strong" form of the principle of verification should be used is too extreme as it rules out the use of verification in principle, and it challenges the sense of the laws of science. Such propositions as "arsenic is poisonous", "all men are mortal", or "a body tends to expand when it is heated", are propositions whose truth "cannot be established with certainty by any finite series of observations." (1970:37)

Ants and Ayer on Analytic and Synthetic Propositions

As we have seen, Ayer argues that the cognitive status and so the meaning of a proposition can be established by analytic and synthetic criteria and that these constitute the "weak" form of verifiability. The key idea here is variously formulated, and the following summary definition by Ferré is worth keeping in mind:

> *"The meaning of a sentence is the method of its verification." (1970:30)*

Analytic truths were self-evident, and on synthetic claims Ayer explains in a discussion with Bryan Magee that he maintained that "unless their truth or falsehood made some observable difference they were not significant." (Magee, 1986:68).

As an example of the distinction between analytic and synthetic propositions, Ayer takes the proposition, "There are ants which have established a system of slavery".

He asks "Is this analytic or synthetic?" It is synthetic, because its truth or falsity cannot be determined simply through a study of the symbols used; we have to study the conduct of ants.

In contrast the proposition "Either some ants are parasitic or none are" is analytic because we don't have to examine a single ant to see the sense, meaning and truth of the proposition - we simply have to understand the function of "either", "or" and "none".

And Ayer reminds us that the analytic proposition "Either some ants are parasitic or none are" provides no information about the actual world. Analytic propositions have this quality; none of them "provide any information about any matter of fact." (1970:79)

They are not meaningless, however, because they give information about the use of **SYMBOLS**, and they reveal the implicit workings of symbolic relations in language-use, against the assumptions of common usage.

For example, the assertion that "if all Bretons are Frenchmen, and all Frenchmen Europeans, then all Bretons are Europeans" says nothing about "any actual matter of fact"; it simply shows what is implicit in the statements "all Bretons are Frenchmen" and "all Frenchmen are Europeans."

Ayer distinguishes the sense that is thus contained in analytic and synthetic propositions from the senselessness of metaphysical utterances. The metaphysician, whether of religious or philosophical disposition, produces statements that, Ayer thinks, "do not describe anything that is capable, even in principle, of being observed". Ayer concludes:

> "No dictionary is provided by means of which they can be transformed into statements that are directly or indirectly verifiable." (1970:14)

Ayer's point is that metaphysicians will not allow that their statements are merely analytic - in which case they say nothing about actuality - but neither is experience permitted to count in an empirical fashion as the test of the proposition.

Ayer uses as an example a dispute between two groups of art experts/ philosophers who have examined a painting that appears, on examination, to "really" be by Goya. The criteria for reaching this view are clear enough.

But if the metaphysicians amongst the experts began to contest whether the painting was objectively real or an idea, a set of perceptions in the consciousness of the observer, Ayer asks,

> "What possible experience could any of them have which would be relevant to the solution of the dispute one way or the other?" (1970:40)

The problem is fictitious.

Ayer suggests that an "empirical hypothesis" has a factual point of reference or content because it has the function of serving as a rule for the "anticipation of experience." Such a statement is "synthetic" and so open to evaluation by the practical principle of verification.

The principle of verification is the expression of the idea that if meaning was relative to analytic or synthetic criteria, then, as noted earlier, one could state that "the meaning of a proposition is the method of its verification", that is, meaning was relative to one or the other of the prescribed forms of verification. This is a good statement of the principle of verification, insofar as it emphasises the need for the appropriate method of verification to be applied.

Verification and Religious Language

Ayer's argued that his analysis showed that theistic language was not literally significant, that it was senseless - thus theistic and religious language was not cognitively significant and no knowable truths could be expressed in such "pseudo-language."

The principle of verification made plain the criteria for meaningful discourse, and, like metaphysical statements such as those examined a moments ago, theistic language entailed claims that failed to meet the criteria.

It seems clear that religious thinkers and religious devotees are unwilling to subject the God of faith to some kind of experimental and empirical test, yet they do not want to rest with the view that their language is no more than of private, subjective, significance, they present the religious interpretation as being expressive of the way reality is.

This is problematic.

Ayer's position implies that the referent of such language can't be proved to exist; nor can he be accorded the probable existence which a positivist verification provides.

Such language is not cognitively significant and is therefore meaningless. The assertions of the theologian

> *"cannot possibly be valid, but they cannot be invalid either. As he says nothing at all about the world, he cannot justly be accused of saying anything false, or anything for which he has insufficient grounds." (1970:116)*

Ayer claims that his conclusion is akin to what is actually claimed by many religious thinkers who conceive of the divine as wholly other and incomprehensible, an object of faith not reason, of "purely mystical intuition" such that cannot be defined in terms that are appropriate to reason. Ayer is certainly right in drawing attention to the similarity between his strictures and the line taken by the apophatic theologians. But Ayer has no comfort for the theist: whatever the theist claims, Ayer wants it to be subject to the criteria of verifiability:

"The theist, like the moralist, may believe that his experiences are cognitive experiences, but, unless he can formulate his 'knowledge' in propositions that are empirically verifiable, we may be sure he is deceiving himself. It follows that the those philosophers who fill their books with assertions that they intuitively 'know' this or that moral or religious 'truth' are merely providing material for the psycho-analyst." (1970:120)

Some Problems with the Principle of Verification

There can be no doubt that the principle of verification has positive application within areas like natural science and its derivatives. And equally, the principle has a clear and humane concern for analysis and clarity which is important in most areas of work and study. But the main problem faced by Ayer and his supporters over the principle of verification involves arriving at a stable definition of the principle itself.

It was soon pointed out that the principle would have to conform to its own criteria to be acceptable, but this proved to be difficult because of the narrow range of permitted meaning that the principle of verification acknowledged. The point was that a range of other "sense experiences" - moral, interpersonal, aesthetic, had significance and meaning for experience and symbol-systems. The principle of verification, with its logical, deterministic, and strictly empirical character, simply ruled these out as areas from which real, as opposed to tautological, subjective or emotive meaning, might be generally derived. Such was the lack of plausibility perceived in this attitude that it meant that the principle of verification was either ignored or just selectively employed in the intellectual world at large, in relation to a wider "experiential" method of verification.

The key problem is that the principle of verification uses analytic and synthetic criteria for meaning and thereby truth. It is accepted that analytic propositions are clearly valid criteria. But synthetic judgments are in effect formalised versions of the usual method of scientific investigation, when a specific theory is tested to establish its validity and to provide predictions for the phenomena in question. Arguably such a method works well within the natural sciences. But must we assume that all other domains of experience and insight are to be validated and approved by this method of verification?

Ferré summarises the point thus:

> "That theological discourse has been shown to be untenable when interpreted as pseudo-scientific explanation does not, it would appear, rule out the possibility of its functioning rationally and legitimately in some other way. Verificational analysis does not recognize any other way, but this may illustrate a shortcoming more in verificational analysis than in theological language." (1970:74)

But more specifically, in relation to the criteria used by the principle, it did not seem that the principle of verification could be formulated to meet them.

Suppose I say that "A proposition is meaningful if and only if, it can be verified by logical analysis and shown to be self-evident or contradictory, or verified by sense experience and empirical testing so that the experiential difference made by what is claimed can be known."

Is this proposition true analytically? Is its truth self-evident? Or is it self-contradictory? Is it an empirical proposition? Will its truth be established a posteriori (from experience)?

The critical view is that however we formulate the principle of verification, it cannot be advanced as being empirically verified. It is one view offered in relation to the empirical fact that there were many different forms of seemingly meaningful discourse. It is offered as a means by which these statements might be discriminated between, classified, and evaluated. But is it is not self-evident that empirical verification is the best fit for all cases.

But neither was the principle of verification analytically true as the definition of meaningfulness. It was simply a view of what legitimate meaningfulness entailed, and as such it could not be pressed exclusively and with integrity as the means by which all meaning was determined. This was problematic in consequence of the claim implicit in the principle of verification that those propositions that failed to conform to the criteria of analytic or synthetic truths were nonsensical: it seemed that the principle of verification was nonsensical by its own standards.

Ayer's response to this has been to accept that the key problem of logical positivism was that it was too ambitious. The problem was that the principle of verification could not be formulated in a water-tight manner. Ayer thus suggests that the principle of verification has the status of a **STIPULATIVE DEFINITION** (Magee, 1986:77). It is thus a statement of methodological and evaluative intent, set out clearly over the domain of experience as a means by which meaning, and scientific meaning especially, may be determined. The implication is then that it is up to others to offer their own methods in competition and/or correlation with the principle of verification. We shall see later how some philosophers of religion took up this challenge.

The Principle of Falsification

The criticisms and qualifications of the principle of verification we noted are added to by a further attack from the philosophical and scientific community, insofar as some philosophers came to dispute the notion that scientific values are best determined and expressed via the empirical means employed by the principle of verification. Instead, the principle of falsification was advanced as a corrective.

In relation to this some two years before Ayer published Language Truth and Logic, a young Austrian scholar, Karl Popper, (1902-1994), produced a study entitled Logik der Forschung (the logic of research) that had considerable influence in the long run.

Popper's book was not translated into English until 1959, when it carried the title The Logic of Scientific Discovery.

In this, as in succeeding studies, Popper developed a radical critique of the conventional view of the methods of scientific research. The traditional view was that the proper method for the scientist to employ was to accumulate some data from observation and experiment; then identify some general features and characteristics of the subject in question; then construct hypotheses, which are tested under further experiment and observation. The resulting evidence would confirm/negate the hypotheses, and thus knowledge advances. This is the method of induction - the development of general laws or principles from particular cases or examples.

Popper is against this as the way that science actually worked best.

Popper's view is well-expressed as the title of one of his other books, Conjectures and Refutations. This book is, Popper suggests, a series of variations on the theme that "we learn from our mistakes."

He cites Oscar Wilde's comment that "Experience is the name every one gives to their mistakes" as expressive of the theme, and goes on to suggest that knowledge in general, and scientific knowledge in particular, progresses "by unjustified (and unjustifiable) anticipations, by guesses, by tentative solutions to our problems, by conjectures. These conjectures are controlled by criticism; that is, by attempted refutations, which include severely critical tests." (Popper 1981 p. vii)

Popper adopts the view that knowledge is finite in character, so always provisional and never certain.

Here the distinction between the falsification principle and that of verification becomes clear.

The principle of verification, which operates by means of the empirical method with a reliance of the method of induction, cannot provide verification of anything other than a provisional kind. Empirical generalisations based on experiment and observation, such as "all swans are white", "all wasps sting", "every snowflake is different", do not have logical proof or increased probability of truth via these or through countless other confirming observations and experiments. All that can emerge is a greater or lesser degree of probability.

But of course just one falsifying case of a black swan, a duplicate snowflake, or a benign wasp gives secure validity to the "not every x is y" style of proposition.

Thus falsification makes clearer the nature of our knowledge and the way in which it changes.

Falsification doesn't provide evidence for the absolute truth of anything, but Popper thinks that it makes clear the way in which we best justify our preferences. It avoids the assumption lurking in the principle of verification that certainty over meaning and truth can be obtained.

The implication of the falsification principle is that a statement has meaning or significance if we can specify some way or a possible state of affairs that might falsify it.

Thus Popper remarks that:

> "A theory belongs to science if it is in principle refutable. A theory which cannot clash with any possible or conceivable event is, according to this view, outside science." (Magee 1986:102)

Popper makes it clear that he does not regard non-falsifiable theories as meaningless or as nonsense - a contrast with the view of the verificationists - it is just that such theories are non-scientific, and, Popper seems to think, such theories are pre- scientific.

Various scholars presented or reviewed employed falsification in considering the issues raised by religious language, but we will look at this in the next chapter.

KEY TERMS

Vienna Circle - Logical Positivism - Principle of Verification - Proposition - Cognitive Status - Analytic/Synthetic Propositions - Strong/Weak Verification - Verification in Practice/Principle - Principle of Falsification - Conjecture and Refutation

SELF-ASSESSMENT QUESTIONS

1. Explain why the thinkers in the Vienna Circle favoured logical positivism.

2. Explain and illustrate the basic idea of the principle of verification.

3. Explain and illustrate the distinction between strong and weak verification.

4. Explain and illustrate the distinction between verification a) in practice and b) in principle.

5. Explain the role of analytic and synthetic propositions in Ayer's version of the principle of verification.

6. Explain the problems a logical positivist might have with the proposition, "The meaning of a proposition is its method of verification."

7. Explain the principle of falsification as set out by Popper.

8. Explain the advantages some see with falsification over verification.

And two A2-style questions:

9. Critically assess the effectiveness of the verificationist's claim that religious language is meaningless.

10. "The principle of falsification shows that religious language is not cognitively significant." Discuss.

FURTHER READING

Ayer (1970) is quite an accessible book and there is a 1990 paperback reprint that is easily available. Ayer's conversation with Magee (1986) is extremely valuable. Magee (1975) also gives a lucid review of Popper's work. Hick (1990) and Charlesworth (2002) are both valuable on the key ideas and the issues arising.

The Problem of Meaning for Religious Language

In the mid-1950s a group of scholars produced a number of influential analyses of the issues raised by religious language with reference to variants of the principles of verification and falsification. Their ideas were developed through dialogue and debate whereby they comment on and criticise each other.

To best appreciate their work it is worth considering first a highly significant contribution made by the philosopher John Wisdom (1904-1993). In a famous study first published in 1944 Wisdom examines the view that verification is relative to the provision of a factual assertion the truth or falsity of which can then be determined. He used the following 'parable' to illustrate a problem he saw with this; the parable needs to be read very carefully.

John Wisdom's Parable "Gods"

"Two people return to their long-neglected garden and find among the weeds a few of the old plants surprisingly vigorous. One says to the other 'It must be that a gardener has been coming and doing something about these plants.' Upon enquiry they find that no neighbour has ever seen anyone at work in their garden. The first man says to the other 'He must have worked while people slept.' The other says, 'No, someone would have heard him and besides, anybody who cared about the plants would have kept down these weeds.' The first man says,

'Look at the way these are arranged. There is purpose and a feeling for beauty here. I believe that someone comes, someone invisible to human eyes. I believe that the more carefully we look the more we shall find confirmation of this.' They examine the garden ... and sometimes they come on new things suggesting that a gardener comes and sometimes they come on new things suggesting the contrary and even that a malicious person has been at work. Besides examining the garden carefully they also study what happens to gardens left without attention. Each learns all the other learns about this and about the garden. Consequently, when after all this, one says 'I still believe a gardener comes' while the other says 'I don't' their different words now reflect no difference as to what they have found in the garden, no difference as to what they would find in the garden if they looked further and no difference about how fast untended gardens fall into disorder. At this stage ... the gardener hypothesis has ceased to be experimental, the difference between one who accepts and one who rejects it is not now a matter of the one expecting something the other does not expect. What is the difference between them? The one says, 'A gardener comes unseen and unheard. He is manifested only in his works with which we are all familiar,' the other says 'There is no gardener' and with this difference in what they say about the gardener goes a difference in how they feel towards the garden, in spite of the fact that neither expects anything of it that the other does not expect." (Wisdom in Santoni 1968: 300-301)

In the parable the facts of the world of experience are not disputed by the two protagonists, so much as the value and meaning of the facts as they individually interpret them. This means that the debate between them over whether there is a gardener or not is not an experimental one. Wisdom thinks the same point applies to the question of religious truth and to the debate between theists and atheists. The real issue has to do with discernment rather than with the facts, therefore verification of empirical facts alone isn't of much value. What is different between theists and atheists is their perspective of reality as a whole, just as the two people in the parable differ in their response to the facts. The contradiction between them is a dispute over interpretation. Both understandings - and all of the language used - involve appeals to experience and to the way of the world. Thus, it isn't so obviously correct to affirm one over the other in the way attempted in the principle of verification. Both provide readings of life with a greater or lesser degree of value, where value is relative to the extent to which the version in question can be argued for and defended from experience.

It can be suggested that there is a case for a wider form of experiential verification for religious, ethical and philosophical views. As in the parable discussed by Wisdom, the interpretation made over the state of affairs influences conduct.

For example, if I see a patch of land as waste I shall treat it one way, but I shall treat it in a rather different way if I see it as a garden. The same goes for the way I see reality as a whole, on the interpersonal, social, cultural and eternal planes. Therefore my religious and ethical faith as expressed through my attitude to life, my actions, and in linguistic form, indicates my response to and interpretation of reality, and that is the point of reference for the meaning of the language concerned. The further point, of course, is to do with whether my view is true. For as in the example, it matters whether the land was waste or a garden, since it matters that my action is appropriate, as I shall seem a fool if it turns out that I was wrong. But as we have suggested above, if empirical verification in the strict sense is inadequate, then a wider and richer form of experiential verification is worth developing.

Falsification and Theism - Flew's Parable of the Two Explorers

The falsification principle was applied to theology by Anthony Flew (1923-2011). It is worth mentioning that for most of his career Flew reasoned that atheism was the most probable and best explanation for reality. Later in life he shocked his atheist friends and his former theistic opponents by arguing that in the light of the latest evidence he now thought the intellectual case for theism was stronger, and so he supported it. Flew's book There is a God (2008) gives his account of this. However, here we consider Flew's earlier incarnation as a philosopher of atheism who was keen to use Popper's principle of falsification to debunk theism and all related religious language.

Flew's test-question to theism was to ask what would have to happen to refute the credibility of theism to such an extent that commitment to belief in God, and thus to the positive use of committed religious language, could not be sustained. Flew thought that it was a feature of theism that nothing would be allowed to count against it, that it was thus a non-falsifiable theory and accordingly a non-scientific and by implication, pre-scientific and obsolete perspective.

To explain his view Flew offers a parable developed from Wisdom's parable 'Gods':

> "Once upon a time two explorers came upon a clearing in the jungle. In the clearing were growing many flowers and many weeds. One explorer says, 'Some gardener must tend this plot'. The other disagrees, 'There is no gardener'. So they pitch their tents and set a watch. No gardener is ever seen. 'But perhaps he is an invisible gardener.' So they set up a barbed-wire fence.

They electrify it. They patrol with bloodhounds. (For they remember how H G Wells' The Invisible Man could be both smelt and touched though he could not be seen.) But no shrieks suggested that some intruder had ever received a shock. No movements of the wire ever betray an invisible climber. The bloodhounds never gave cry. Yet still the Believer is not convinced. 'But there is a gardener, invisible, intangible, insensible to electric shocks, a gardener who has no scent and makes no sound, a gardener who comes secretly to look after the garden which he loves.' At last the Sceptic despairs. 'But what remains of your original assertion? Just how does what you call an invisible, intangible, eternally elusive gardener differ from an imaginary gardener or even from no gardener at all?'" (Flew in Santoni, 1968: 315-316)

Flew argues that the Believer and the Sceptic move from original assertions to contrasting "picture preferences". The facts are not in dispute - it is a matter of interpretation. However, the qualifications introduced to supposedly support the Believer's position actually dissipates it, so the "hypothesis may thus be killed by inches, the death by a thousand qualifications" (p. 316).

Flew's presentation is further illustrated via the hypothetical case of the child who is dying of cancer, in relation to the love of the heavenly father, within which it seems that nothing will count against the belief in this deity, despite its non-intervention on behalf of the child, which is what the earthly father's love entails, (1968:317-318). Flew's point is that it is easy to specify what might cause us to abandon the view that we were actually loved by a person. If we get nothing but abuse from that person and letter bombs through the post, then it is a fair bet that love is no longer the best way to describe our relationship.

Flew is doubtless mindful of the analogy traditionally held to exist between human and divine love, which perhaps implies that the same form of falsification might, by analogy, entail a test of faith. But the view reached by Flew is that in fact nothing is permitted to refute the mysterious love of God. A near miss is thought to signal the protection of God; injury is indicative of the care of the divine in contrast to worse consequences; death is relief from further suffering - but this is the "death of a thousand qualifications."

R M Hare, Lunatics, Dons and Bliks

In discussion with Flew and Mitchell (see below), R M Hare (1919-2002) responded with another parable which involves a lunatic and some dons - Oxford slang for university tutors:

> *"A certain lunatic is convinced that all the dons want to murder him. His friends introduce him to the mildest and most respectable dons, and after each of them has retired, they say, 'You see, he doesn't really want to murder you: he spoke to you in a most cordial manner; surely you are convinced now?' But the lunatic replies 'Yes, but that was only his diabolical cunning; he's really plotting against me the whole time, like the rest of them; I know it I tell you.' However many kindly dons are produced the reaction is still the same." (1968:318)*

Hare reasons that as the lunatic refuses to allow anything to count against his view, his theory on Flew's grounds asserts nothing that can be counted as significant. But Hare points out that there is, in fact, a difference between what the lunatic thinks about dons and what the rest of those involved think. This is evident from the fact that the lunatic is called a lunatic, whilst his friends are sane and the dons are understandably worried.

Hare then introduces one of the more memorable terms to have entered debates in philosophy of religion; the **BLIK**. By a "blik" Hare means a perspective that we just have, a "given" of our outlook. Thus Hare suggests that we characterise our sane view of dons as a sane blik whereas the lunatic has an insane blik.

Hare gives another example: he drives a car and he acts on the blik that the car will respond to the movements he imparts via the steering wheel. He knows that this is something that could go wrong - steering mechanisms do fail sometimes - but nevertheless Hare operates on the blik of driving on the assumption that the steering will be reliable. It is possible to imagine that one might have another blik - one that involved cars and steering mechanisms that regularly broke. This might give rise to another blik resulting in an aversion to cars. However, Hare thinks that we can't change our blik. Hare won't change his blik even if the steering fails on a given occasion; in contrast, the person who has the blik that no steering is safe won't be persuaded by all the times that it is.

Hare thus concludes that with our outlooks or dispositions:

> *"Our whole commerce with the world depends on our blik about the world; and that differences between bliks about the world cannot be settled by observation of what happens in the world." (1968:319)*

Hare makes a further point against Flew. In Flew's parable, he thinks that the two explorers are detached in their attitude towards the garden - they discuss it "with interest, but not with concern." In contrast, Hare's lunatic cares about dons just as Hare himself cares about the steering of his car. Hare's view is that Flew has not been able to provide an explanation in his parable of this aspect of experience. Hare thinks he as done more to penetrate the view that it is the disposition exhibited by a blik that is the basis for what we (with that blik) will accept and allow to count as an explanation of experience.

For example, I might have the blik that everything that happens in world happened by pure chance. Hare points out that this "would not, of course, be an assertion; for it is compatible with anything happening or not happening" (p. 320). Hare points out the contrary view (that things happen for reasons) is just as compatible with everything. There will however, be a big difference between how you live if a.) you have the blik of pure chance or b.) the blik of things happening for reasons. It is this that discloses the real differences between what it is to be religious or not to be religious.

Hare is suggesting that it is the blik that counts, not assertions or propositions the truth or meaning of which can be definitively given. So the issue about religious truth and knowledge is not linguistic but experiential and, we might say, existential.

Hare is moving towards a **COHERENCE** view of truth (although he does not call it that), the view that a theory is right (or more likely to be right) if it coheres with other views. Thus the blik of pure chance is not coherent - it means you can't plan or expect anything. The contrary blik (things happen for reasons) is much more coherent. Hare's idea is then that the issue for the religious blik is to do with its coherence in relation to other perspectives on life.

Mitchell's Parable of the Resistance – the Partisan and the Stranger

The philosopher Basil Mitchell (1917-2010) offers another parable constructed to explore further the problems of religious understanding. Mitchell's point is that the key to understanding the theological position is the perspective of faith. The theologian is committed to trust God and so for that reason and by that faith won't allow anything to count ultimately against God. Theologians agree with Flew that evil and suffering count against Christian faith, but also argue that it won't count ultimately.

To illustrate this Mitchell's parable runs as follows:

> "In time of war in an occupied country, a member of the resistance meets one night a stranger who deeply impresses him. They spend that night together in conversation. The Stranger tells the partisan that he himself is on the side of the resistance - indeed that he is in command of it, and urges the partisan to have faith in him no matter what happens. The partisan is utterly convinced at the meeting of the Stranger's sincerity and constancy and undertakes to trust him.
>
> They never meet in conditions of intimacy again. But sometimes the Stranger is seen helping member of the resistance, and the partisan is grateful and says to his friends, 'He is on our side.'
>
> Sometimes he is seen in the uniform of the police handing over patriots to the occupying power. On these occasions his friends murmur against him: but the partisan still says, 'He is on our

side.' He still believes that, in spite of appearances, the Stranger did not deceive him. Sometimes he asks the Stranger for help and receives it. He is then thankful. Sometimes he asks and does not receive it. Then he says, 'The Stranger knows best.' Sometimes his friends, in exasperation, say, 'Well, what would he have to do for you to admit that you were wrong and that he is not on our side?' But the partisan refuses to answer. He will not consent to put the Stranger to the test. And sometimes his friends complain, 'Well, if that's what you mean by his being on our side, the sooner he goes over to the other side the better'" (Mitchell in Santoni, 1968:321-323)

Mitchell makes the following points about his parable and its relationship to the matters raised by Flew and Hare:

1. The partisan does not allow anything to count against the Stranger. This follows from and expresses his commitment of trust in the Stranger. This is expressed in the assertion of faith "The Stranger is on our side." However, he does see that the Stranger's behaviour sometimes counts against his faith, and it is this that makes a challenge to him, and to his belief.

2. The partisan admits that things count against his faith in the Stranger and this shows the conflict that the partisan feels and that his faith is held openly - things are allowed to count against it.

This contrasts with Hare's idea of bliks. The lunatic, we recall, won't allow anything to count against his view that all dons are murderers. The lunatic has no sane reason for his blik, whereas the partisan has reason for his commitment to the Stranger. Mitchell also wants to say that the partisan's belief about the Stranger is an **EXPLANATION**:

> *"It explains and makes sense of the Stranger's behaviour; it helps to explain also the resistance movement in the context of which he appears. In each case it differs from the interpretation which the others put upon the same facts." (1968:323)*

Mitchell suggests that "God loves men" resembles "the Stranger is on our side." These statements, and historical statements (like "Richard III was killed on the field of battle at Bosworth") are not conclusively falsifiable (or verifiable, of course).

Mitchell then argues there are three possible ways of dealing with such statements:

1. "As provisional hypotheses to be discarded if experience tells against them".

2. "As significant articles of faith".

3. "As vacuous formulae (expressing, perhaps, a desire for reassurance) to which experience makes no difference and which make no difference to life".

Mitchell concludes:

> *"The Christian, once he has committed himself, is precluded by his faith from taking up the first attitude: 'Thou shalt not tempt the Lord thy God.' He is in constant danger, as Flew has observed, of slipping into the third. But he need not; and, if he does, it is a failure of faith as well as of logic." (1968:323)*

John Hick and Eschatological Verification

In his book Faith and Knowledge John Hick (1922-2012) argues for a theologically orientated version of the verification principle.

In keeping with the tradition started by Wisdom's parable "Gods" Hick employs a philosophical parable to communicate his key point.

> *"Two men are travelling along a road. One of them believes that it leads to a Celestial City, the other that it leas nowhere; but since this is the only road there is, both must travel it. Neither has been this way before, and therefore neither is able to say what they will find around each new corner. During their journey they meet with moments of refreshment and delight, and with moments of hardship and danger. All the time one of them thinks of his journey as a pilgrimage to the Celestial City and interprets the pleasant parts as encouragements and the obstacles as trials of his purpose and lessons in endurance, prepared by the king of that city and designed to make him a worthy citizen of that place when at last he arrives there. The other, however, believes none of this and sees their journey as an unavoidable and aimless ramble. Since he has no choice in the matter, he enjoys the good and endures the bad. But for him there is no Celestial City to be reached, no all-encompassing purpose ordaining their journey-only the road itself and the luck of the road in good weather and in bad." (Hick, 1974:177)*

Hick wants to convey the following ideas with this parable:

- Religious language can be verified and can be seen as

meaningful and factually significant. Here Hick agrees in principle with Ayer's demand for verification.

- Hick agrees with the idea that for a propositional statement and for the belief(s) connected to it to be meaningful it must be factually significant - and this means that the truth or falsity of the proposition must make a difference to us and to our experience of the world.

- Hick also agrees with Ayer that the most appropriate thing to do is to seek verification of the propositions concerned.
  Hick introduces an important clarification of what verifiability must include; this is the idea that effective verification is what delivers a removal of reasonable doubt about the matter in question. This is because the questions of the truth or falsity of the religious view of life is not a purely logical problem. If it were, the matter would rest on logical analysis alone.

Hick takes as basic to his view the idea that as a matter of fact it is a feature of the religious perspective in of Christianity that there is belief in an after-life, in some form of post-death experience. The eventuality of this after-life would, Hick proposes, remove any rational doubt about the truth-claims of Christianity. Hick draws on a remark of Moritz Schlick's to support this proposal:

> *"We must conclude that immortality in the sense defined, (i.e. 'survival after death' rather than 'never-ending life') should not be regarded as a 'metaphysical problem' but as an empirical hypothesis, because it possesses logical verifiability. It could be verified by following the prescription, 'wait until you die.'" (1974:179)*

Hick terms this **ESCHATOLOGICAL VERIFICATION** (1974:180). This is the key term he introduced into this whole area of debate. Eschatology is a term drawn from New Testament theology which relates to theories about last things and judgment. Hick's idea is that Christian faith entails an intrinsic expectation of judgment and so it is a part of the logic of faith to live with that in mind. If we are to rightly assess the coherence of the religious language of such a faith, then we have an inbuilt criterion for verification.

KEY TERMS

The Philosophical Parables: 'Gods' (Wisdom) - The Two Explorers (Flew) - The Lunatic and the Dons (Hare) - bliks - The Partisan and the Stranger (Mitchell) - The Two Travellers (Hick) - Eschatological Verification

FURTHER READING

The various philosophical parables have been widely anthologised. Santoni (1968) packages them well but Flew and MacIntyre (1955) remains the classic. Ferré (1970) is an excellent guide on the wider issues and Hick (1990) and Charlesworth (2002) are both reliable and thoughtful.

SELF-ASSESSMENT QUESTIONS

1. Explain clearly what Wisdom's parable "Gods" says about the case for factual verification.

2. What problems does the religious language user face from Flew's presentation of the "two explorers"?

3. Illustrate and explain Hare's notion of bliks.

4. Explain and illustrate the implications of Mitchell's "The Partisan and the Stranger" for the religious language debate.

5. Explain and illustrate Hick's proposal for "eschatological verification".

6. Imagine you are A J Ayer and write a challenge against the arguments of Hare, Mitchell and Hick.

7. Write notes on the ways in which the principle of falsification might impact on the arguments of Hare, Mitchell and Hick.

8. Reviewing the material examined in this and the preceding chapter write notes on what sorts of evidence or information can be derived from religious language.

And two A2-style questions:

9. Evaluate the view that the meaning of religious language is given by faith.

10. Assess the view that the logic of religious language is dependent on eschatological verification.

Myth, Symbol and Religious Language

RELIGIOUS LANGUAGE AND MYTH

Within Theology and the discipline of Religious Studies, the concepts of myth and mythology have tremendous significance. The terms do not suggest legends or fantasies, rather, the view is that in religious traditions, including Christianity, Buddhism, and Islam, texts, narratives and traditions exhibiting mythic form can be found. Examples of mythical narratives within the biblical literature include the Creation narratives in Genesis, and the birth narratives in Matthew and Luke. In this context, myths are textual versions of earlier oral traditions where fundamental questions of meaning, purpose or value were explored. Myths thus reflect explorations of fundamental concerns about human destiny in ways that relate to historical existence as, in part at least, interpretations of what is perceived to be the truth of it.

From this we must see that in the setting of theological discussions and in the context of the study of religion, "myth" denotes a story or narrative which may have some basis in history; historical accuracy and detail in the modern sense are not the key focus, however. The myth will use metaphors or parabolic teachings or symbols, analogies or allegories to present insights, truths and understandings that have to do with fundamental questions of meaning and purpose.

A key function of myth is that the narratives provide inspirational and motivational readings of the moral vision for life.

Another is that myths provide an indirect means of expressing or interpreting something of the infinite and inexpressible "Holy".

Myths are important to students of religion as well as to those within the religions in questions because the they appear to represent insight into fundamental problems that are characteristic of the religion in question, and characteristics of the tradition of faith within that religion back to that religions earliest times. Myths thus predate theology, doctrine, philosophy and so on. One implication of this is that mythical understanding is via faith rather than through theological interpretation or reflection.

However, myth should not be seen in isolation from the other aspects of religion. In a number of his writings, Ninian Smart develops an influential phenomenological view of religion, which is what is in evidence when the **SEVEN DIMENSIONS OF RELIGION** are present:

1. **MYTH** - narratives expressing and exploring fundamental questions of meaning, being, value and truth.

2. **RITUAL** - patterns of ceremony and worship, devotions expressive of the faith and belief characteristic of the religion - mythic narratives may be re-enacted in devotional rituals, cf. Eucharist.

3. **DOGMA** - doctrines, teachings, principles and theories constituting the theology and philosophy of the tradition in question. The ideas here may be expressed in myth and ritual.

4. **ETHICS** - principles for the practice of life, moral values and principles for how life is to be fulfilled. Mythic and allegorical writing may explore and present the ethical principles.

5. **EXPERIENCE** - the experiential dimension of religion might entail the special or distinctive experiences the religion involves or it may denote the particularity of engagement with the religion through all of the dimensions.

6. **SOCIAL** - the communal aspect of the religion. This may be closely linked to the experiential and ritualistic dimensions.

7. **MAYERIAL** - the physical aspects of religion within an historical and cultural tradition; buildings and shrines and the like. (See Smart, 1998)

What we need to appreciate from Smart's definition is that Myth is a key component of what "Religion" is.

A vital feature of myth follows from the fact that the language of myth is infused with images, metaphors and symbols - and so the idea that a literal or factual meaning is here relevant is a major mistake. Nevertheless, it is a mistake commonly made within religious traditions and by the critics of religion. From both camps we will find evidence of arguments that assume that mythical writing is to be taken literally. Fundamentalists thinkers in Judaism, Christianity and Islam will not like to see various narratives in the Old Testament defined as "myth" as this will be too close to the idea that they cannot be true, and contemporary atheists such as Richard Dawkins' dislike the idea of myth in case it leads to the possibility that they might be.

BULTMANN: DEMYTHOLOGISING THE NEW TESTAMENT

Another significant contribution to the discussion of religious language as "myth" comes from the New Testament scholar Rudolph Bultmann (1884-1976). He argues that it is appropriate to describe the mind-set of the first-century as exhibited in the texts of the New Testament as "mythological" (See Bultmann 1958). He means by this that the world-view assumed by the writers of the New Testament is one infused by spiritual realities and powers, by forces and agencies that are how reality is for the age in question.

> *"The whole conception of the world which is presupposed in the preaching of Jesus as in the New Testament generally is mythological, i.e., the conception of the world as being structured in three stories, heaven, earth and hell; the conception of the intervention of supernatural powers in the course of events; and the conception of miracles, especially the conception of the intervention of supernatural powers in the inner life of the soul, the conception that men can be tempted and corrupted by the devil and possessed by evil spirits." (1958:15)*

In a recent work, J. M. Robinson suggests that the "Temptations" narrative found in Matthew and Luke, where Jesus is confronted by the devil, is the **MYTHICAL EXPRESSION** of Jesus' historical wrestling with the question of what sort of mission he should embark upon (Robinson, 2007:68). Thus, the texts are written to convey a reading of reality as understood in the context of composition. For the modern reader, the texts include much that runs counter to what we take to be common sense, and what we assume as viable from the scientific and anthropological point of view. For example, biblical cosmology describes the earth in a suspended state above the murky world of Sheol and beneath the heavens; evil spirits from below and divine influences from above invade "our world" in a cosmic battle. This is a pre-scientific but sacred view of reality, "wrong" to us, but the key point is, normal in the time of writing.

The world-view of the Gospel of Mark is a classic example of this sort of mythology: think of the instances of demon possession, of healing via the casting out of spirits, of the relation between disease, sin, healing and forgiveness (See Mark 1.22 - 5 for example).

Bultmann's idea is that we need to "demythologise" the New Testament: thus we do not judge it directly via the intellectual criteria of modernity; we need to re-interpret the mythic world-view and the texts composed under its assumptions, by working our way into the human situations that the myths address, so that we can gain an understanding of the message about the human condition that the texts deal with. Bultmann thinks that we are able to examine a mythic text - the birth stories in Luke and Matthew, for example - and by unpeeling the mythical layers we disclose within the narrative a sense of the reality of God's purpose being fulfilled through the lowly and the excluded - "the humble are exalted".

In similar manner, Bultmann points out that in the First Century in Hellenistic culture, it was common to have a myth of a redeemer of heavenly origin or significance who is killed and resurrected. His argument is that in Christian experience this myth is attached to the historical Jesus and writers from Paul onwards express an eschatological version of the resurrection myth to prepare the followers of "the way of the Lord" for the judgment that is believed to be at hand, (1958:16).

Bultmann thinks it is clear that this whole mythical structure is to us an anachronism and so taken literally it is of no significance; but "demythologised", the resurrection stories are express the transformation of the self that occurs through the commitment of faith. Bultmann argues the need to demythologise so as to negotiate the problem of cultural relativism.

A problem with this is that we can argue that there is always the difficulty of accurate translation as we deconstruct a myth from a prior age and seek to reconstruct its meaning for modernity. Of course, we might say that this is a major problem only if we undertake the business of translation on isolated occasions; if we made a coherent effort we are likely to be able to make a much more accurate job of it.

PAUL TILLICH AND LANGUAGE AS SYMBOL

To link the discussion of myth to the consideration of religious language as symbolic, we can look at what Paul Tillich (1886-1966) says in linking the language of symbols with the concept of myth.

Thinking of classical Greek mythology Tillich writes that:

> *"Myths are symbols of faith combined in stories about divine-human encounters." (Tillich, 2009:56)*

Myth is present "in every act of faith, because the language of faith is the symbol."

> Myth *"uses material from our ordinary experience. It puts the stories of the gods into the framework of time and space although it belongs to the nature of the ultimate to be beyond time and space ... it divides the divine into several figures, removing ultimacy from each of them without removing their claim to ultimacy. This inevitably leads to conflicts of ultimate claims, able to destroy life, society and consciousness." (2009: 56-57)*

In his view of the relation between myth and symbol Tillich is emphatically critical of Bultmann's idea of "de-mythologizing" the biblical narratives. Myth and symbol must remain as they are "forms of human consciousness which are always present. One can replace one myth by another, but one cannot remove the myth from man's spiritual life. For the myth is the combination of symbols of our ultimate concern." (2009:58)

We will consider Tillich' idea of **ULTIMATE CONCERN** in a moment. On myth and symbol Tillich argues that a danger is literalism - the habit of treating myth and symbol as having literal, factual meaning. This is a defence mechanism that comes in the face of the fear of de-mythologising. In a view that anticipates much of more recent experience, Tillich thinks that the fear of the orthodox is that the liberal critique of religious expressions will result in a defence of orthodoxy that becomes more literal and more fundamentalist and thereby, anti-intellectual and ill-disposed to rational scrutiny and development.

Religious Language as the Language of Symbols

There is a close link between considering the language of religion as myth and considering it as symbolic.

John Macquarrie (1919-2006) explains the relation of symbols to myth:

> "In myth itself, the symbol and that which is symbolised have not yet been clearly distinguished. As soon as we recognise a symbol as a symbol, we have taken a step back from the myth and emerged from a purely mythological way of thinking and talking. Thus although it is often said that myth is indispensable to the expression of religious truth, this statement is not accurate. What is meant is that religious or theological language cannot dispense with symbols, specifically, the symbols drawn from myth ... But the fact that these symbols are now understood as symbols and that they can be discussed and illuminated in an alternative interpretative language indicates that the person who can handle them in this way has transcended a merely mythical apprehension of the symbols." (Macquarrie, 1966:122)

Macquarrie's point is to endorse the idea of the mythic mode of expression that we find in religious traditions, and then to suggest that the key images - the symbols - that are embedded in myth are in fact the key theological motifs that we need to review and which can be "discussed and illuminated" in linguistic mind sets other than that of the original.

The idea that the language of religion should be considered significant as a form of symbolic expression is developed by a number of scholars: two who are particularly influential are J.H. Randall (1899-1980) and again, Paul Tillich.

J. H. Randall's ideas are set out in The Role of Knowledge in the Western World (1958).

Randall portrays religion as:

1. A natural phenomenon

2. A human activity

3. A culturally vital activity

Randall suggests that just as art opens up our appreciation of beauty, so Religion via its symbols opens up the possibilities for moral and communal life, indicating the ways in which humans can transcend how they are and move towards what they can be.

Religious Symbols are said to have four particular functions:

1. To **ENGAGE** the core emotions of people and so inspire them to actions within common ethical values.

2. To **STRENGTHEN** and **SUSTAIN** communal and cooperative actions.

3. To **COMMUNICATE** values that transcend the literal and the self.

4. To **REFLECT** and **DEFEND** the aspect of reality we call "divine".

For Randall "God" is "an intellectual symbol for the religious dimension of the world, for the divine" (1958:112). We should be clear that he sees "God" as a socio-cultural intellectual construct, a view that draws on a variety of earlier naturalistic studies of religion, such as those by Feuerbach and Durkheim. Nevertheless, Randall endorses religion within and for human experience, and his view is to promote a broad view of the domains of understanding humanity can employ. He is anti-reductionist in the sense that he opposes reducing all meaning to the criteria of empirical science; but he is not defending a realist view of religious truth.

Signs and symbols

In his book Dynamics of Faith (first published in 1957) Tillich makes a distinction between signs and symbols: he uses the familiar concept of a traffic light as the illustrative example. The traffic light is a sign:

"It points to the order to stop the movement of cars at certain intervals." (2009:47)

Thus the traffic light points beyond itself. Tillich says that all signs point "beyond themselves." This is also the first characteristic of symbols, but one that they share with signs. However, Tillich thinks that the sign has no essential relationship to that to which it points.

The relationship of the red light to the job of pointing up the command to "Stop" is, Tillich suggests, a convention that could be changed.

In a key move Tillich says that "signs do not participate in the reality of that to which they point, while symbols do." (p. 48)

Thus a second key feature of a symbol, and the one that is said to make it distinct from a sign is that it "participates in that to which it points".

Tillich takes as his example the flag of a nation. He was writing in the USA and so he had in mind the Stars and Stripes; we might think of London 2012 and the occasions when the Union Jack was flown to signal Gold Medal success for Team UK, or of Wimbledon 2013 and the flags waved to celebrate and share in the victory of Andy Murray. Tillich's idea is that for a people, a nation, the flag participates in the "power" and the "dignity" of the nation for which it stands.

Tillich claims that the participation of the flag in that to which it points means that 'it cannot be replaced except after a historic catastrophe that changes the reality of the nation which is symbolises.'

Tillich is almost certainly thinking here of the symbol of the Swastika and the post- War situation where The Federal Republic of German and the German Democratic Republic had new flags, until the further transformation of the reunification of Germany in the early 1990s, when another new flag emerged.

Tillich suggests four further characteristics of a symbol that distinguishes a symbol from a sign.

The first two are as follows:

5. Symbols "opens up levels of reality which otherwise are closed for us" and that;

6. symbolic language "also unlocks dimensions and elements of our souls which correspond to the dimensions and elements of reality." (p. 49)

Tillich thinks, for example, that the arts all employ symbols to open up reality in a distinctive way: a picture or poem can portray reality in way that is distinct from a biologist or geologist. And a great novel or play might give us "not only a new vision of the human scene, but it opens up hidden depths of our own being … There are within us dimensions of which we cannot be aware except through symbols, as melodies and rhythms in music."

7. The fifth aspect of symbols is that they "cannot be produced intentionally". Symbols have a "social function", they grow from the "individual or collective unconscious" and they cannot operate "without being accepted by the unconscious dimension of our being."

8. A sixth characteristic of the symbol is that they "grow and die": a symbol grows within and for a situation that is **RIPE** and symbols **DIE** when that situation fades away.

Tillich takes the symbol of "king" as a classic case of a once potent symbol that is far less active and so far less significant for the modern period. Tillich argues that the life and death of a symbol has nothing to do with human longing or the advances of scientific and historical understanding. Symbols die "because they no longer produce responses in the group where they originally found expression", (p. 50).

Tillich on Religious Symbols

On the basis of his distinction between sign and symbol and his explanation of symbols in general Tillich moves to consider the nature and role of religious symbols.

Two key statements are these:

> *"The language of faith is the language of symbols." (2009:51)*

> *"… faith, understood as the state of being ultimately concerned, has no language other than symbols." (2009:50-51)*

As we might infer from the above, Tillich defines "faith" as state of "ultimate concern" with God as the object or "content" of the ultimate concern. Here it is vital to understand how Tillich distinguishes matters of preliminary concern, meaning our everyday concerns, from matters of ultimate concern.

Tillich asks rhetorically why it is that we can't express faith as ultimate concern "directly and properly?" (p. 50)

Tillich then notes that a variety of things might be the focus of a person's faith, as that which is the focus for a "state of ultimate concern": he considers "success" and "the nation".

We can unpack the idea of "the nation" becoming a person's ultimate concern. Here Tillich is almost certainly mindful of what had happened in

Germany in the 1930's as Nazi ideology became a dominant form of nationalism with a religious or quasi-religious fervour.

Suppose the nation becomes someone's ultimate concern:

> *"The name of the nation becomes a sacred name and the nation receives divine qualities which far surpass the reality of the being and functioning of the nation. The nation then stands for and symbolises the true ultimate, but in an idolatrous way." (2009:50-51)*

Similarly with "success" - still a potent motivator in our contemporary experience;

> *"Success as ultimate concern is not the national desire of actualizing potentialities, but is readiness to sacrifice all other values of life for the sake of a position of power and social predominance. The anxiety about not being a success is an idolatrous form of the anxiety about divine condemnation. Success is grace; lack of success, ultimate judgement. In this way concepts designating ordinary realities become idolatrous symbols of ultimate concern." (2009:51)*

Tillich then makes explicit his key argument:

> *"The reason for this transformation of concepts into symbols is the character of ultimacy and the nature of faith. That which is the true ultimate transcends the realm of finite reality infinitely. Therefore, no finite reality can express it directly and properly. Religiously speaking, God transcends his own name. This is why the use of his name easily becomes an abuse or a blasphemy. Whatever we say about that which concerns us ultimately, whether or not we call it God, has a symbolic meaning. It points beyond itself while participating in that to which it points."*

Some Problems in seeing Religious Language as Symbolic

Against Randall, we noted how Randall's ideas reflect an anti or non-realist view of "God". The term "God" does not denote a reality - "God'"is an expression of human imagining, an expression of human values and concerns.

Many religious believers and thinkers dislike this notion. John Hick argues (see Hick, 1990:87) that we take the affirmation made by theists that "God is Good", it matters here that God is in some sense "Good" and that the phrase "God is Good" is not wholly symbolic.

Against Tillich, Tillich is often criticised for his attempt to distinguish between signs and symbols. Tillich is perhaps handicapped by being a native German speaker. He left Germany in 1933 at the age of 47 and began a new life teaching in America and having to adopt English as the language of communication for his lectures. He does not seem to appreciate how, in use, we might say "These clouds are a sign of snow" where the clouds really do have an intrinsic link with that which is signified. Mathematical and logical symbols, on the other hand, are altogether more arbitrary in their relation to the functions that they stand for. So clouds are said to be signs but they "participate in the reality of that which they point to", and mathematical symbols appear not to participate in the reality of the functions to which they arbitrarily point. We might add that Tillich is on questionable ground when he says that the red traffic light has no intrinsic relation to that to which it points - the necessity of stopping. "Red" is surely a generic cultural symbol for danger? Wouldn't this make replacing 'red' a very difficult thing to do?

Macquarrie (1966:123-126) thinks that the importance of symbolic language is such that we can't abandon it - but he thinks that Tillich's sign/symbol distinction is too clumsy.

Macquarrie suggests the following distinction as a corrective:

▸ Conventional Symbols

Here we find an arbitrary link between the symbol and that to which it points. Symbols on a TV remote control might be "conventional" in this sense.

▸ Intrinsic Symbols

Here there would be a relation of "kinship" between the symbol that that which it symbolised. The wine in Eucharist would have "kinship" and this would, for the Christian adherent, involve an "existential response" of faith and an understanding of a "similarity of relation."

Further to this we should stress that many scholars have questioned Tillich's idea that symbols are distinctive because they "participate in the reality of that to which they point."

The concern is with the sense and meaning of the term **PARTICIPATION**. We discussed this earlier with the flag of the nation, and the question of how the flag operates to share or participate in the dignity and power of the nation.

Tillich's use of the notion or participation is of course neo-Platonic (all goods participate in the Form of the Good) and is also based in the Judaeo-Christian notion of creation - the creation expresses and participates in the life and reality of the creator. Tillich uses the notion of participation to put into what we might term counter-poise the religiously significant aspect of life that thereby becomes an active religious symbol: in such a symbol we need an "element of concreteness'"which is taken from our experience and applied "symbolically to God" and the "element of ultimacy" that is not symbolic and which the symbol also expresses. In this sense the symbol "affirms and denies itself" and it is this that signals participation.

The problem remaining is that Tillich clearly aims to use participation as a key to defining the symbolic nature of religious language, with participatory symbols being distinguished from arbitrary and conventional signs. Yet in his Systematic Theology Tillich argues that:

> *"Without participation the category of relation would have no basis in reality." (1968:196)*

Tillich means by **RELATION** ways in which relationships operate - the "knower participates in the known", the "lover participates in the beloved", the "existent participates in the essences". It seems that in this usage **PARTICIPATES** overarches both **SYMBOL** and **SIGN** and suggests that Tillich has not adequately sustained a clear distinction between them.

SELF-ASSESSMENT QUESTIONS

1. Write clear notes to define the theological and religious concept of myth.

2. Research and assess Bultmann's project of "demythologising" the New Testament.

3. Check and collate ideas to explain the relationship between myth and symbol.

4. Write clear notes on the functions of symbols as understood by Randall.

With Tillich's theory, make sure you have clear notes and examples on:

5. How signs and symbols work with one common characteristic and how they differ.

6. The five further characteristics of symbols.

7. Religious symbols as symbols of ultimate concern.

8. The problem of participation - and other problems for Tillich's theory.

And two A2-style questions:

9. Assess the claim that is myth an effective way of conveying religious truth.

10. "Religious language is devalued if it is only symbolic". Discuss.

KEY TERMS

Myth - Demythologising - The Functions of Symbols (Randall) - Sign/Symbol Distinction (Tillich) - Six Characteristics of Symbols (Tillich) - Ultimate Concern - Conventional and Intrinsic Symbols (Macquarrie) - Participation and its Problems

FURTHER READING

Tillich (2009) - a new edition of Dynamics of Faith - is a classic text. Hick (1990) and Charlesworth (2002) are very reliable guides.

Wittgenstein, Meaning and Truth

AN INTRODUCTION TO WITTGENSTEIN

A pervasive interest in recent philosophy has been with problems of meaning and truth with a particular emphasis on the nature and workings of language. In this context Ludwig Wittgenstein, who we mentioned briefly earlier, is distinctive for having produced two influential, but competing philosophies. The first is embodied in the only philosophical book he published in his lifetime, Tractatus Logico-Philosophicus (1921). His second philosophy emerged from his work from about 1929 and is set out particularly in Philosophical Investigations, a text he worked on for some years before his death and which appeared in 1953.

Wittgenstein is one of the most significant of all philosophers. Born into an affluent family in Vienna he, by some remarkable events and decisions too detailed to relate here, spent five terms between 1911-1913 at Cambridge working with Bertrand Russell (1872-1970), who shared with G.E. Moore (1872-1958) and the economist John Maynard Keynes (1883-1946) the view that in Wittgenstein they had a true philosophical genius in their midst. At the outbreak of war in 1914 it was clear that Wittgenstein was on his way to producing a major work. The work was in draft form when Russell and Wittgenstein met in 1919. In 1921 it was published in a German journal and the next year it was published in Britain. On the suggestion of G E Moore, the book was given the title Tractatus Logico-Philosophicus - it is now generally known as the Tractatus.

The Tractatus and the Picture Theory of Meaning

The Tractatus was admired by the Vienna Circle. What they liked is what is usually called the **PICTURE THEORY OF MEANING**.

Wittgenstein finds fascination in the fact that language can function in such a way as to enable meaningful communication. The problem, he thinks, is that of the possibility of language. How is meaningful language possible? We are all conscious of the extent to which language can mislead or blur meaning, but the presupposition of this consciousness is an awareness of the effective power of language to operate as a vehicle of meaning by means of which issues can be presented and resolved - issues from the mundane to the profound. Wittgenstein is profoundly interested in the basic fact that language has the potential to work to the extent that we are able, as in everyday conversations or activities, to grasp the sense and meaning of sentences and propositions that we have never seen or heard before.

In the Tractatus (which is written in decimally notated propositions not in extended prose) Wittgenstein seeks to show that a limit to language can be demonstrated, as can the real limits of reality. The limits - and they are said to be correlated - once disclosed will show that many philosophical problems arise and are insoluble because they aim to pass beyond the limits of reality, thought and language. Thus the Tractatus' message - enigmatically apophatic - is that

> *"what can be said at all can be said clearly, and what we cannot talk about we must pass over in silence." (Wittgenstein, 1961:3)*

In the Tractatus the proposal is that language works because there is a relationship between the form and structure of language and the form and structure of reality. Basic to linguistic activity, Wittgenstein implies, is ostensive definition - **NAMING** - thus a given word stands for a specific thing, and thus the fundamental components of language stand for basic elements in reality, which they name. Accordingly, the possibility of language is grounded in the fact that true linguistic propositions - statements that say something that we understand - convey a picture of reality - a picture of the world as it is or as it could be. The link between language and reality by means of which language conveys effective sense about reality is created through the picturing operation of language. Language provides a picture which shows its sense and, Wittgenstein thinks, an analysis of the elements of the picture reveals a correspondence with the elements of reality - the character and shape of reality can thus be derived from an analysis of language.

Wittgenstein is clear that this view may seem strange. A proposition printed on a page, he remarks, "does not seem to be a picture of the reality with which it is concerned." (4.011) But he suggests that neither does musical notation appear at first sight to be "a picture of a piece of music" nor does the alphabet seem to be "a picture of our speech". Wittgenstein's point is that the correspondence, the picturing, is logical not photographic. He says in the Tractatus: "Logic deals with every possibility and all possibilities are its facts". (2.0121) He argues that the potential in language to truthfully represent and communicate what is the case is based in a correspondence between the elements in the structure of the world and the basic components in language.

Propositions are said to picture facts. Thus the picture theory of Wittgenstein's Tractatus is grounded in the view that logically names denote objects - "A name means an object. The object is its meaning" (3.203) - and combinations of names form elementary propositions, which reflect the combinations of objects in and as states of affairs - "The simplest kind of proposition, an elementary proposition, asserts the existence of a state of affairs" (4.21). Here the logical pattern of elementary propositions mirrors the arrangement of objects in and as **STATES OF AFFAIRS** - "The configuration of objects in a situation corresponds to the configuration of simple signs in the propositional sign" (3.21) - and thereby propositions picture facts and thus language and reality correspond to enable meaningful language.

Just as a relief or contour map models an area of terrain, so the logical structure of language pictures the structure of reality.

A picture, Wittgenstein says, "is a model of reality" (2.12).

He continues:

> *2.13 In a picture objects have the elements of the picture corresponding to them.*
>
> *2.131 In a picture the elements of the picture are the representatives of objects.*
>
> *2.14 What constitutes a picture is that its elements are related to one another in a determinate way.*
>
> *2.141 A picture is a fact.*
>
> *2.15 The fact that the elements of a picture are related to one another in a determinate way represents that things are related to one another in the same way.*

Wittgenstein terms the connexion of the elements of a picture its **STRUCTURE** and the possibility of this structure "the pictorial form of the picture".

PICTORIAL FORM here "is the possibility that things are related to one another in the same way as the elements of the picture." (2.151)

Thus:

- That is how a picture is attached to reality; it reaches right out to it (2. 1511).

- It is laid against reality like a measure (2. 1512).

This analysis provides the framework for what is, and what is not the case, and what in consequence can and cannot be said:

> *"In order to tell whether a picture is true or false we must compare it with reality". (2.223)*

With these ideas in place it was no surprise that members of the Vienna Circle, as discussed earlier, thought Wittgenstein was on their side. Wittgenstein takes, in conjunction with the analytic truths and tautologies of logic and maths, the language and approach of natural science as being the determinative approach for authentic language - language that depicts reality through pictures or models that can be compared with reality through checks and tests. Thus "Reality is compared with propositions" (4.05) and, 'A proposition can be true or false only in virtue of being a picture of reality.' (4.06) Wittgenstein considers that this view sets the limits and conditions for authentic language. His claim is that to be set meaningfully within language the subject of a proposition has to be set within reality as an actual or possible state of affairs. However, if a statement fails to express a proposition - a picture of something in (or claimed to be in) the world - then it fails to say anything that could be true or false, and such a statement is nonsense. Wittgenstein suggests that most of the problems of philosophy are nonsensical in this manner. They aim to advance to a metaphysical statement about the nature of things as such and as a whole, but such a move entails a shift beyond the common limits of language and reality.

So how is it that Wittgenstein thought (rightly) that the Vienna Circle had misunderstood him?

The Tractatus and the Mystical

We cited earlier a comment from the Preface of the Tractatus: "what can be said at all can be said clearly" it ran, and we can see that this is a guide to the picture theory of meaning. But it continued, "what we cannot talk about we must pass over in silence." Note the phrasing: Wittgenstein means there are matters we cannot talk about, and these we must not try to talk about, but stay silent over. These matters turn out to matter a lot to Wittgenstein. In the last few pages of the Tractatus Wittgenstein makes a number of remarks about **ETHICS**, the **MYSTICAL** and to "what is higher". He mentions ethics, (6.421), "the sense of the world", (6.41), "the world of the happy ... and ... the unhappy." (6.43), the "riddle of life", (6.4312) and God, (6.432). He reflects on the problem of life and he writes about problems and ideas that would be unintelligible to the Vienna Circle.

He says, for example:

> 6.432 "How things are in the world is a matter of complete indifference for what is higher. God does not reveal himself in the world."

> 6.44 "It is not how things are in the world that is mystical, but that it exists."

6.45 *"Feeling the world as limited whole - it is this that is mystical."*

6.52 *"We feel that even when all possible scientific questions have been answered, the problems of life remain completely untouched. Of course there are then no questions left, and this itself is the answer."*

6.521 *"The solution of the problem of life is seen in the vanishing of the problem. (Is not this the reason why those who have found after a long period of doubt that the sense of life becomes clear to them have been unable to say what constituted that sense?)"*

6.522 *"There are, indeed, things that cannot be put into words. They make themselves manifest. They are what is mystical."*

These remarks suggest a religious concern and an ethical sense, but one that has an apophatic character of extreme proportions.

In this context, it is important to consider some comments of Wittgenstein's in a letter to his friend Ludwig Von Ficker written at about the time of the Tractatus' publication.

Wittgenstein writes that:

"The book's purpose is an ethical one. I once meant to include in the preface a sentence which is not in fact there now, but which I shall write out for you here, because it will perhaps be a key to the work for you. What I meant to write, then, was this: My work consists of two parts: the one presented here plus all

that I have not written. And it is precisely this second part that is the important one. My book draws limits to the sphere of the ethical from the inside as it were ... I have managed in my book to put everything in its place by being silent about it." (LW to LvF in McGuiness 1988:288)

This remark is typical of others Wittgenstein made to friends suggestive of a far from negative attitude to the ethical and religious dimensions of experience - but his point is really that the ethical is a condition of experience not something that exists as a part of the world of experience: ethics and one's faith can't be spoken about, but they can be done.

Wittgenstein and the Philosophical Investigations

▶ Word as Deeds

In 1929 Wittgenstein decided to return to Cambridge. He had thought that the Tractatus had solved all of the problems of philosophy that mattered, but time, and perhaps the logical positivists, persuaded him there was more to do. From 1929 to his death in 1951 Wittgenstein worked intensively and produced a mass of material. The book that emerged first, Philosophical Investigations, represents a small percentage of work, but the themes it presented have had great influence.

The Philosophical Investigations dramatically provides one of the most famous criticisms of the Tractatus, dramatic since it stems from Wittgenstein himself. The Tractatus presents the picture theory of meaning. But Wittgenstein later saw that this was misleading in relation to the phenomenon with which it deals - language. The Tractatus suggests that all language has a common essence disclosed through its logical structure. In the later philosophy Wittgenstein repudiates this view. His assertion "Words are ... deeds" (1953:546) encapsulates the new insight that language is composed of a diverse range of activities and functions which exhibit meaning, sense and value - and in those contexts a style and logic - relative to circumstance and use.

The point is that in the Tractatus naming, or **OSTENSIVE DEFINITION**, is regarded as the basis of meaning in language. In the later philosophy reliance on this explanatory model is rejected. The range and diversity of the functions of language is seen to extend far beyond ostensive definition. Questioning, commanding, promising, obeying, and so on, exhibit meaning and involve sense, but such functions do not name and do not picture facts and are not helpfully elucidated through the analysis prescribed by the Tractatus. Thus whilst the Tractatus assumes that the world is full of complexes analysable into their constituent parts and simples - the objects - and language is thus a corresponding structure scaling down to names, Wittgenstein's later philosophy sees language and reality as a more dynamic phenomenon, with degrees of meaning relative to use and context. In Philosophical Investigations, whilst Wittgenstein specifically retains an interest in the same issues as he considers in the Tractatus, he now challenges the view that propositional or picturing modes of meaning are determinative of all linguistic sense and the aspiration to prescribe the formal general theory of the essence of language as a whole.

Language and the Purpose of Philosophy

Philosophical Investigations suggests that there is error in seeking a single logic for language, that such attempts manifest a serious misunderstanding of language; the error involves looking for the meaning of language instead of at the meaning in language.

Wittgenstein remarks that "Philosophical problems arise when language goes on holiday" (38); confusions arise "when language is like an engine idling, not when it is doing work." (132)

Wittgenstein also suggests that philosophical problems can be dissolved through a therapeutic approach:

"The philosopher's treatment of a question is like the treatment of an illness.' (255) It is the aim of philosophy to 'shew the fly the way out of the fly-bottle." (309)

He means that misunderstanding follows from a consideration of language when it is removed from its practical context or when it is examined through some abstract criteria, as when we attempt to establish the order of language against some "preconceived idea to which reality must correspond" (131). Such analysis and explanation leads to the "dogmatism into which we fall so easily in doing philosophy", and must be replaced by 'description' of the possible orders of language. Thus philosophy "simply puts everything before us, and neither explains nor deduces anything." (126)

The problems of philosophy are solved:

> "by looking into the workings of our language, and that in such a way as to make us recognise those workings: in despite of an urge to misunderstand them." (109)

The philosopher's task therefore involves an arrangement or rearrangement "of what we have always known." Consequently philosophy is "a battle against the bewitchment of our intelligence by means of language."

As an investigation into the problems of philosophy, Wittgenstein suggests that the investigation is "a grammatical one", (90). It seeks to remove misunderstandings which arise through too great a focus on **SURFACE GRAMMAR**, by which Wittgenstein means the style of meaning and the sense that we anticipate finding in expressions when we are bewitched into thinking that all meanings operate in a particular way. In contrast we should look for the **DEPTH GRAMMAR**, the variety of sense and meaning that is disclosed in and through actual language. (See 664).

Language Games and Forms of Life

The best-known image Wittgenstein employs in his theory is the term **LANGUAGE-GAME** which he introduces in a diffuse manner. He suggests that the games through which we learn our native language - pointing, repeating, naming - are language-games, as is the primitive language that enables such other games to mean something. He also calls "the whole, consisting of language and the actions into which it is woven, the 'language-game'." (7)

A sense of the key meaning here derives from a passage a little later in the text:

> *"The term "language-game" is meant to bring into prominence the fact that the speaking of a language is part of an activity, or of a form of life." (23)*

Wittgenstein likes the analogy with games because he sees that all games - he refers to "board-games", "card-games", "ball-games" and the "Olympic games" (66) - are practical, active and indeed interactive, and they are all rule-governed. Language use, is, the thinks, just like this. He then invites us to consider the multiplicity of language-games in the following examples:

- "Giving orders and receiving them
- Describing the appearance of an object, or giving its measurements
- Constructing an object from a description (a drawing)
- Reporting an event
- Speculating about an event
  Forming and testing a hypothesis

- Representing the results of an experiment in tables and diagrams
- Making up a story; and reading it
- Play-acting
- Singing catches of a song
- Guessing riddles
- Making a joke; telling it
- Solving a problem in practical arithmetic
- Translating from one language into another
- Asking, thanking, cursing, greeting, praying. (23)

Ostensive definition is "a language-game on its own" (27) but there is within language (and life) a great variety of language-games. Consider what can be done with exclamations - Wittgenstein offers another list:

- 'Water!
- Away!
- Ow!
- Help!
- Fine!
- No!' (27)

Of the various language-games that can be observed Wittgenstein wryly comments,

> "It is interesting to note the multiplicity of the tools in language and of the ways they are used, the multiplicity of kinds of word and sentence, with what logicians have said about the structure of language. (Including the author of the Tractatus Logico-Philosophicus)" (23)

By linking the idea of language games to that of forms of life Wittgenstein is giving his theory an anthropological and social character, as he says "What we are here supplying are really remarks on the natural history of human beings." (415)

The examples at the start of this book - going to the football match, cheering, singing, chanting - going to the church, kneeling and praying - these are **FORMS OF LIFE** and there are languages games particular to each, as well as some that overlap. One might sing at a football match and sing in Church; these overlaps Wittgenstein terms **FAMILY RESEMBLANCES** (67). Going back the various games we mentioned earlier, all card-games have in virtue of using cards, family resemblance, as do all team sports in virtue of having teams, all racquet sports in virtue of using racquets, and so on. Wittgenstein's idea is that in a similar way, our language games within forms of life show this **RESEMBLANCE**.

Meaning and Use and Meaning and Truth

In Philosophical Investigations Wittgenstein suggests that,

> *"For a large class of cases - though not for all - in which we employ the word 'meaning' it can be defined thus: the meaning of a word is its use in the language" (410).*

He advises that we should, "Let the use of words teach ... their meaning. (Philosophical Investigations II xi p. 220 - Part II of Philosophical Iinvestigations is arranged in numbered sections and the convention is to refer by page number).

We find Wittgenstein employing the following vision of words and their sense to convey the new view:

"Think of the tools in a tool-box: there is a hammer, pliers, a saw, a screw-driver, a rule, a glue-pot, glue, nails, screws. The functions of words are as diverse as the functions of these objects. (And in both cases there are similarities.)" (11)

The key idea here is "The functions of words are as diverse as the functions of these objects". Wittgenstein's example is a box of tools, and we may use one of the tools mentioned metaphorically to say that here Wittgenstein deals a hammer-blow to the logical positivists. It will be recalled that they argued that via the principle of verification the ability to affirm or negate the truth of a proposition determined its meaning. On this method, truth is prior to meaning.

Wittgenstein's "meaning as use" theory reverses this: meaning derives from use, so the question of meaning is prior to the question of truth; what is "true" will be relative to meaning which is relative to use.

An implication of this approach is that if meaning is relative to use then the criteria for truth for a given language game will be established within the meanings and usage of that language game. With regard to religious language questions arising from this new approach were raised. For example, is there a **RELIGIOUS LANGUAGE GAME**, or games, with variations in terms of **FORMS OF LIFE** and **FAMILY RESEMBLANCE**? What, if anything, did Wittgenstein think?

Wittgenstein on Religion and the Meaning of Life

In his writings Wittgenstein makes many references to religious or philosophical issues. In his early period we have seen that in effect he writes with an implicit apophatic stance as some things cannot be said but only shown through action and commitment.

In the later work it might seem that he could argue that the language of faith could be expressed as a distinct language-game, as a clear form of life. In fact Wittgenstein does not do this in the Philosophical Investigations. After his death his literary executors found a mass of carefully ordered manuscripts, many of which in due course have been published. From this material some insights can be found into Wittgenstein's ongoing view about religion, the meaning of life, and the possibility of giving this expression.

In notes he made when reading Frazer's The Golden Bough, a multi-volume anthropological study of magic and religion published between 1890 and 1915, Wittgenstein is critical of Frazer who he sees as falsely assuming that religions provided hypotheses and theories about reality, analogous to but manifestly inferior to the more modern sciences. Wittgenstein says that Frazer's account of magical and religious traditions is unsatisfactory because "it makes these views look like errors."

Wittgenstein then remarks,

> "Was Augustine in error, then, when he called upon God on every page of the Confessions? But - one may say that - if he was not in error, surely the Buddhist holy man was - or anyone else - whose religion gives expression to completely different views. But none of them was in error, except when he set forth a theory." (Wittgenstein 1993:119)

What Wittgenstein seems to mean by the meaning, truth and so the point of a religious point of view is suggested in some remarks collected in the book Culture and Value (1980). Wittgenstein suggests that religious commitment is really all about a way of being, a way of reacting or responding to the world. It is a distinctive, unique and irreducible style of commitment:

> "A religious belief could only be something like a passionate commitment to a system of reference. Hence, although it's belief, it's really a way if living or a way of assessing life. It's passionately seizing hold of this interpretation." (Wittgenstein, 1980:64e)

Although Wittgenstein did not elaborate a theory of how religious language might work, it was not long before others applied aspects of his theory to the problem of religious language. We will consider two: R.B. Braithwaite and D.Z. Phillips.

▸ **Braithwaite - The empirical meaning of religious language**

Richard Braithwaite (1900-1990) studied with Wittgenstein at Cambridge in the 1930s. He specialised in mathematics and the philosophy of science and he developed a response to the problem of religious language in a lecture, "An Empiricist's View of the Nature of Religious Belief", given in 1955.

As we may recall, Wittgenstein makes the case in Philosophical Investigations for the view that "the meaning of a word is its use in the language." (1953:43) Braithwaite approaches the issue of religious language by affirming that he does not intend to consider ethical or religious language as language to be categorised as cognitivist, as language to be analysed on a framework of literal or factual truth. Nor is he keen to agree with the logical positivists that ethical language is purely emotive. Rather, Braithwaite proposes a non-cognitivist view where the question of truth is thus subordinate to the question of meaning, and, following Wittgenstein, the view presented is that the meaning of language is expressed via the user and the usage determines the meaning.

Braithwaite states that "the meaning of any statement ... will be taken as being given by the way it is used." (Braithwaite in Santoni, 1968, p. 333)

Explaining this, Braithwaite says his view is **CONATIVE** not emotive. (p. 334) By conative he means that his view will be related to the intentions expressed in the language - the intention, the will to act in a certain way, is the indicator of meaning. Whilst feeling is a key aspect of moral assertions and all that follows from them, Braithwaite does not think it is the most significant aspect. The key thing is the users "intention to perform the action."

Braithwaite then affirms that "the primary use of a moral assertion is that of expressing the intention of the asserter to act in a particular sort of way specified by the action."

As an illustration, following Braithwaite's exposition, if we consider a utilitarian's assertion of acting well to maximise happiness we know that what this means is that this utilitarian is intending to act so as to bring about the greatest happiness to the greater number. Considering the assertion in this way is, Braithwaite argues, helpful as it gives us something that the emotivist could not provide, namely, a way of explaining how the user could think that he had reason to make the assertion - or that he has a reason for the action, thus is it wasn't just emotive. The reason for the action to the user is that he intends to do it so as to maximise happiness, all other things being equal.

Turning to religious language and to assertions made in that context, Braithwaite thinks that is clear from the vast literature that exists on religious and theological matters that religious language has to do with emotion and feelings, such as the feeling of harmony between the self and the universe. But he thinks that for religious people the language of faith is about more than just feeling. It is a common feature of religious self-understanding that a person's commitment will be demonstrated through action. Therefore Braithwaite says that "the intention of a Christian to follow a Christian way of life is not only the criterion for the sincerity of his assertions of Christianity; it is the criterion for the meaningfulness of his assertions." (p. 336)

Braithwaite's next move is to consider an objection. If we take a moral assertion, such as the proposal that "I am going to act so as to tell the truth and not be a liar", the resolution to so act presupposes that I know what it is to lie and what it is to tell the truth. It is not problematic to set out the empirical facts concerning these policies. But what about religious assertions? How are we to know the worth of the policies specified by the religions to which we affirm allegiance? This is an issue, of course, for example, for those of Ayer's disposition who consider that the legitimacy of both metaphysical and theological utterances has been wholly eroded.

Braithwaite's solution to this difficulty is in effect to promote a coherence view of truth. He thinks that the assertions of a distinctive religion are a part of a larger body of assertions that collectively constitutes the religious system in question. The particular assertions are therefore to be "taken by the asserter as implicitly specifying a particular way of life."

Braithwaite thinks that the matter is in fact analogous to what happens in science:

> "We understand scientific hypotheses, and the terms that occur in them, by virtue of the relation of the whole system of hypotheses to empirically observable facts; and it is the whole system of hypotheses, not one hypotheses in isolation, that is tested for its truth value against experience. So there are good precedents, in the empirical way of thinking, for considering a system of religious assertions as a whole, and for examining the way in which the whole system is used." (p. 337)

As might be guessed from the remarks made above, Braithwaite then puts focus on the sense in which religious assertions have a moral function - as in "specifying a particular way of life". To deny this, he argues, would require the mediation of a moral assertion between the assertion of the religious view and the intention to follow the policy of action in question. However, the **INTENTION-TO-ACT** concept of moral and religious assertions requires no other reason to explain why a religious person acts morally. This view of religious assertions "is the only view which connects them to ways of life without requiring an additional premiss."

Braithwaite thinks it is clear that within Christianity the assertion that **GOD IS LOVE**, - agape, as in I John 4:8 - is the epitome of Christian assertions and that it connects directly to the intention "to follow an agapeistic way of life."

Braithwaite then explains how empirical testing can be applied to interrogate the asserter of such a view to see whether other consistent and coherent principles are expressing the systematic view of the religion as typically understood. And we would observe the actions of the asserter to examine the extent to which they were consistent with the assertions made as statements of intent. Here the maxim of "actions speaking louder than words" fits the case.

We thus come to the most commonly cited passage from Braithwaite:

> "the primary use of religious assertions is to announce
> allegiance to a set of moral principles: without such allegiance
> there is no 'true religion'." (p. 338)

Braithwaite adds that the religious commitment is a "state of the will" - emphasising the conative nature of his view as mentioned earlier.

Braithwaite anticipates the criticism that he has reduced religious to moral assertions, and he is keen to argue that this is not his purpose. He suggests that there are distinctive empirical features of religious as opposed to moral assertions; religious assertions are a part of a system - moral assertions might not be; religious assertions are not abstract - they are related to concrete examples, such as Christian teachings, parables and so on in the case of the assertion of Christian commitment. And religious assertions imply an implicit as well as an explicit aspect; there is a concern for the inner life of the asserter, for reflection, as well as for the active side:

> "The conversion involved in accepting a religion is a conversion,
> not only of the will, but of the heart. Christianity requites not
> only that you should behave towards your neighbour as if you
> loved him as yourself; it requires that you should love him as
> yourself. And though I have no doubt that the Christian concept
> of agape refers partly to external behaviour - the agapeistic

97

behaviour for which there are external criteria - yet being filled
with agape includes more than behaving agapeistically
externally: it also includes an agapeistic frame of mind." (p. 339)

Braithwaite thus thinks we can empirically distinguish religious from moral assertions.

How do we distinguish particular religions?

Braithwaite thinks that each religious system is characterised by its own particular stories or sets of stories, and he says that for the Christian the intention to follow the agapeistic way of life is associated with thinking of particular sets of stories. In this sense, we might say, the assertions of the Christian is a form of the "imitation of Christ." Braithwaite thinks that there will be variations of types of Christian assertion, but that they will all be empirically testable. By the same methods, we can identify and measure other religious traditions.

Briathwaites' allegiance to Wittgenstein comes through again when he argues that on the view he has developed it is not necessary "for the asserter of a religious view to believe in the truth of the story involved in the assertion; what is necessary is that the story should be entertained in thought, i.e. that the statement of the story should be understood as having a meaning." (p. 342) The meaning is more vital than the truth and what Braithwaite sees is that religious stories have a psychological and inspirational force that can shape and direct action:

"A religious assertion ... is the assertion of an intention to carry
out a certain behaviour policy, subsumable under a sufficiently
general principle to be a moral one, together with the implicit or
explicit statements but not the assertion, of certain stories." (p.
345)

Problems with Braithwaite's view

One major question is raised against Braithwaite: is it accurate and is it legitimate to cast into the role of intentional statements of an ethical character all religious assertions?

Religious people are not only making ethical statements when they express in devotional or theological terms statements of faith. Some statements may be referential, relating to the nature of reality, the divine (however conceived) or to the self as a means to the end of obtaining a clearer insight. Braithwaite's reference to the "implicit" meaning of religious language is his acknowledgment of this aspect - but is it sufficient? A Christian might say that they use theological and religious language in prayer and other devotions to express faith in God (who is eternal), reality (regarded as Creation) and life (seen as a gift of grace). Our Christian might say that all this language has meaning but that it has meaning because in or through faith it is expressing truth. Braithwaite argues of course, that his is a non-cognitivist view, and here he is being a faithful interpreter of Wittgenstein's relativistic theories of language games and forms of life in Philosophical Investigations. But if we stick with the case of Christian faith, our Christian might say that Jesus' characteristic teaching was not, as a matter of historical fact, just of an **AGAPE ETHIC**. It a lot to do with the tensions between of living with and for, or without and against God: John Hick writes on this that:

> "Jesus was a realist; he pointed to the life in which the
> neighbour is valued equally with the self as being indicated by
> the actual nature of the universe. He urged people to live in
> terms of reality ... Whereas the ethic of egoism is ultimately
> atheistic, Jesus' ethic was radically and consistently theistic. It
> sets forth the way of life that is appropriate when God, as

99

depicted by Jesus, is wholeheartedly believed to be real." (Hick 1990:95-96)

If Christian faith assertion make in effect factual claim about reality, it is not adequate to reduce them to non-cognitive terms as Braithwaite does.

Another more technical criticism of Braithwaite concerns his assumption that an ethical assertion signals the intention to act in an ethical way. This sounds good in theory, but it can be argued that we do not always find that ethical assertions are universally consistently applied. What people say when they assert **ETHICAL INTENTIONS** is one thing, what they actually do is another, and whether it is ethical and consistent with the intention would surely be a third matter for consideration. This suggests that Braithwaite's theory lacks precision.

RELIGIOUS LANGUAGE AS A LANGUAGE-GAME

D.Z. Phillips (1934-2006) wrote extensively on Wittgenstein's later philosophy, applying the language game theory to Christian understanding in particular. He was not as wholly relativistic as the later Wittgenstein became, as he thought that what he termed the 'cool place' of Philosophy, was that it had a classical concern with basic questions about reality. He means that the presupposition for philosophical investigation is that there is a reality to examine and describe. He asks rhetorically how philosophy can:

> *"give an account of reality which shows that it is necessary to go beyond simply noting differences between various modes of discourse, without invoking a common measure of 'the real' or assuming that all modes of discourse have a common subject, namely, Reality?" (Phillips 1999 :11)*

One of Phillip's most famous studies considers the tensions in Christian faith between immortality and eternal life, Death and Immortality (1971). A key point is that it is a common view within Christianity that immortality is the promise the faithful have as the mode of life after death.

There is no doubt at all that this view is as a matter of fact a matter of Christian belief and teaching. This had led to a mass of philosophical debate about the nature of the soul, the meaning of immortality and the cognitive status of such propositions on every side of the debate. Phillips thinks such debates are in fact mistaking the rules of the real language-game that is truly relevant to the issues. The problem is that these terms are used if they denoted something substantive, something essentially real and true.

Phillips, following Wittgenstein, does not think religious concepts have that kind of status anyway. If we look at the mode of discourse in the key narratives in the New Testament, Phillip's point is that debates about the immortality of the soul is not a topic we find in the characteristic teachings of Jesus. What we find there is a focus on 'eternal life' as a way of living within "this life".

Let's explore this. In Luke 10.25 a Lawyer is portrayed as asking what he must do 'to inherit eternal life?' In Mark 10.17 a rich man asks the same question of Jesus. If we look hard at the answers Jesus actually gives we find that to the Lawyer Jesus affirms that he must follow the teaching of the Law; in summary "You shall love the Lord your God with all your heart, and with all your soul, and with all your strength and with all your mind; and your neighbour as yourself." In Luke's narrative the Lawyer asks a supplementary question, "Who is my neighbour?", and this gives Luke the opportunity to unleash the parable of the Good Samaritan (Luke 10.30-35). When that is told, Jesus asks the Lawyer (who has asked, "What must I do to inherit eternal life?" and "Who is my neighbour?"), "Who was neighbour to the man who fell into the hands of the robbers?", he turn in the question here is highly significant, as it re-orientates the direction of enquiry. The Lawyer replies "The one who showed him mercy." Jesus' reply is "Go and do likewise." And the point is that this is the answer to both of the Lawyer's questions: eternal life is living a certain way towards others now and for the future. The answer to the rich man is strikingly similar. The man is told to keep the commandments. He says he has kept them "… since my youth." (Mark 10.20) Jesus then tells him the one thing he needs to do is to "sell all that you own, and give the money to the poor." (Mark 10.21) The man will then "have treasure in heaven" and can become a follower of Jesus. Again, the entailment of eternal life is living in a different and qualitatively distinct way now and for the future.

In effect Phillips is using insights into strands of contemporary New Testament studies as well as his insight into Wittgenstein to argue that a language-game of one kind – soul theory and immortality - is mistaken and that another - living eternal life - is correct. Eternal life is not, in Phillips' view, something that comes into play for the faithful after death. Eternal life turns out to be the way the faithful could and should be living now and the language of eternal life is thus expressive of the affirmative commitment to that way of being where faith and hope are real aspects rather than belief in the immortality of souls.

An issue for the use of Wittgenstein's language game theory is that, despite what Wittgenstein says about family resemblance, it seems that each language game runs by its own rules and values. This suggests that there are criteria for a given language game or form of life - say that of Philip's view on eternal life - that are distinct from the rules for the language games (or "forms of life") of orthodox Catholicism, or of sceptical determinism, each of which will have very distinct takes on souls, immortality and eternal life. The implication of arguing that truth is relative to meaning, and meaning relative to use, is that no overarching criteria for use, meaning or truth can be appealed to. Just an emotivist in ethics can give no reasons for saying that "Nazi genocide is morally wrong", so on the operating system of the later Wittgenstein, it is hard to say of, for example, the Nazi language game, that it was morally and intellectually wrong. Thus a key problem is how to live with intellectual security with this degree of relativism. We noted that Phillips thinks that philosophy is in a "cool place", avoiding this problem, but it is not clear how exactly he can use Wittgenstein's approach and avoid this, and so the risk is, perhaps, that philosophy's place just got hotter.

SELF-ASSESSMENT QUESTIONS

1. Write clear notes on how the picture theory of meaning works.

2. Illustrate and explain the different implications of ostensive definition and definition of meaning via use.

3. Illustrate and explain the idea of language games. Develop your own examples.

4. Writing a dialogue between the early and later Wittgenstein to show the contrasting views of what can be said.

5. Write a clear and illustrated summary of Braithwaite's theory of religious language.

6. Write out key arguments to use to review and criticise Braithwaite.

7. Write a clear and illustrated summary of Phillips' theory of religious language.

8. Write out key arguments to use to review and criticise Phillips.

And two A2-style questions.

9. Evaluate the view that Wittgenstein's theory of language games allows for religious language to be considered significant.

10. Critically assess the view that the 'the primary use of religious assertions is to announce allegiance to a set of moral principles'.

KEY TERMS

Ostensive Definition - The Picture Theory of Meaning - Pictorial Form - The Mystical - Word as Deeds - Language Games - Forms of Life - Family Resemblance - Conative and Emotive Meaning - Religious Language having Expressive Ethical Intention (Braithwaite) - Religious Language Games (Phillips)

FURTHER READING

Genova (1995) and Pears (1971 and 2006) are excellent on Wittgenstein. Hick (1990) and Ferré (1970) are again very helpful. Charlesworth (2002) gives a valuable overview. Wittgenstein's own works are well worth exploring: Culture and Value (1980) is a good place to start.

Verification and Paradox Revisited

In this final section two further contributions to the religious language debate are considered. I.T. Ramsey (1915-1972) and I.M. Crombie (1917-2010). Both made important inputs to the arguments we have been considering.

In 1957 Ramsey published Religious Language, a text that remains as one of the most frequently consulted studies of the topic in question.

RAMSEY ON RELIGIOUS LANGUAGE

Ramsey's view is that religious experience is empirically measurable; religious language expressive of this distinctive experience is coherent, meaningful and valid.

Ramsey's main ideas can be put under the following four headings:

1. Being is the presupposition for language

Rather like Braithwaite, but in a much more deliberate manner, Ramsey seeks to reply to the charges made by the Logical Positivists that religious language was meaningless as it could not be verified. Against this Ramsey thinks a substantial response is possible, as indicated by his book's subtitle, "An Empirical Placing of Theological Phrases".

Ramsey begins by arguing that the basis for religious language is a religious life. The life of a religious person is a state of faith and a condition of commitment. It is a commitment within and for reality. In relation to this, religious language is expressive and reflective - but the key thing is that propositional arguments do not have a great deal of significance. Ramsey's point is that it is an empirical fallacy to think that there are evidential grounds for thinking that religious belief rests on the validity of linguistic propositions.

We can follow an example Ramsey offers (Ramsey, 1957:40-42). Suppose a man, Smith, gets up one day at 4 a.m. and it turns out he was made to do this so this was not a free action. Suppose on another occasion he gets up again at 4 a.m. at his own volition. We inquire why and he explains "I wished to have breakfast early", so as to "catch a bus", and this because he wanted to "go fishing". If we ask "Why do this?" we get the answer, "What a question! You know what fishing is to me. Fishing is fishing."

The last tautology, "fishing is fishing", is not meaningless: Ramsey's point is that it is a **MEANINGFUL TAUTOLOGY** that communicates an expression of the intrinsic commitment felt for fishing for the life of Smith. Whether we approve of fishing or not, the meaning is clear.

Now let's adapt Ramsey's example. Suppose a person, Lucy, gets up at 4am. Why? "To go to pray." Thus the action, (getting up), is the consequence of a commitment (to praying). Language serves to express that prior commitment. If we ask "Why do this?" Lucy might say, "Prayer is prayer!" Again, this is meaningful tautology that communicates an expression of the intrinsic commitment felt for prayer by Lucy. Whether we like or approve of prayer, the meaning is clear.

Ramsey's point is that the language of religious commitment makes empirical and experiential sense. Thus for the religious person,

> *"'God' is a key word, an irreducible posit, an ultimate of*
> *explanation of the kind of commitment he professes." (1957:47)*

2. The Irreducible 'I'

Ramsey argues that the concept of the self is analogous to the concept of God. If we try to capture in words a total and complete, wholly exhaustive definition of the self, the "I" that we all tend to assume we each are, we get into trouble. We can characterise individual selfhood in a variety of ways, but we will see that even the sum total of descriptions of a person's character is not the same as the "I" within. It is a safe bet that we are all sure that we each are more than the collective view the rest have of us. This shows us that there are expressive limits to the ways in which we can express some ideas and experiences.

Ramsey thinks that we cannot, in human language, capture and express directly God, the mysteries of creation, the nature of freedom and the matters of love and salvation and so on. What is expressed is, in various ways, faith and commitment to these things. Thus "God":

> *"is to be talked about in terms of the object-language over*
> *which it presides, but only when this object- language is*
> *qualified: in which case this qualified object-language becomes*
> *also currency for that odd discernment with which religious*
> *commitment, when it is not bigotry or fanaticism, will necessarily*
> *be associated." (1957:47)*

3. Discernment

Ramsey has a key insight in linking the idea of a person's religious commitment to underlying insight or discernment. This discernment, he argues, discloses the religious understanding that religious language then expresses. Ramsey likens this to the colloquial moment of new insight we express with the phrase "when the penny drops". (1957:49ff) Ramsey's point is that we all have moments in our development, in our learning, when a **TRANSFORMATIONAL DISCERNMENT** occurs. In mathematics, we might have been taught that 3+3=6; we might have been shown on a number of occasions that 3+3=6. But then, at some point, we understand that 3+3 cannot not be 6. Ramsey's idea is that the faith commitment is similarly a transformational discernment that evokes commitment - and this is the basis for the meaning and sense of much religious language.

4. Models and Qualifiers

Ramsey offers a means by which religious language can be understood via an operational analysis of what happens when we say something about our faith in God. No less than earlier scholars and in keeping with the views of most biblical writers, Ramsey is sure that it is impossible to express direct or literal knowledge of God. On the other hand we use human language to express our faith. How can we use everyday language from the physical world to express something of what we have by way of faith in and commitment to that which transcends the everyday world?

Ramsey's idea is that what happens is that we take a term from everyday language as 'model' for the sort of thing we are trying to express about our faith, and we apply a term as a qualifier to indicate that what we express is not a part of the everyday world, (see p. 49-89). We might, for example, have terms such as wise, loving or good as models for expressions of our sense of God; we then have qualifiers like "eternally", "wholly" or "infinitely" to signal that here we do not mean the literal meaning of the term used as a model, that here the literal meaning is being transcended. There is negation and affirmation going on. We can summarise below the key ideas Ramsey has on this:

MODEL	QUALIFIER
Models are literal, partial and relative ...	*Qualifiers signal depth, mystery, otherness and the absolute ...*
Wise	Infinitely
Good	Eternally
Loving	Wholly

Against Ramsey

Ramsey's attempt to ground religious language in framework that is empirically verifiable is widely respected as having achieved a lot to provide a reading of such language that clarifies its sense.

The problem is, does this achieve a convincing defence of the idea that such language has a reference beyond the experience of the subjects who use the language?

It is one thing to say, like we might of poem, that it is expressive of the experiential commitments that we have. But we will see the poem as a powerful truth via fiction.

Ramsey shows us what is going on with religious language, but does he show us that religious language is also expressing truths about the nature of things?

Or is he showing us the only way that such truth can be expressed?

A study of the concept of revelation for another theme on this philosophy of religion course will enrich a consideration of Ramsey's ideas.

I.M. CROMBIE AND THE POSSIBILITY OF RELIGIOUS STATEMENTS

Ian Crombie was a lecturer in Philosophy at Oxford University. Crombie develops a defence of the meaningfulness of religious and theological language reminiscent of the apophatic style but in a manner that links to the use of **ANALOGY** and paradox. He thus offers a way of combining several of the traditions we have previously examined. Crombie presented his key ideas in a paper entitled "The Possibility of Theological Statements" published in Faith and Logic, edited by Basil Mitchell, in 1957. (See Mitchell, 1957:31-83)

Crombie: First Considerations

What do we mean by "theological statements"?

Crombie means statements expressing beliefs that have an objective and factual status and that are characteristically Christian. Crombie is clear that to be a Christian is to have a commitment to certain beliefs and these beliefs have a factual character - they pertain to reality as it is or was, and in relation to these beliefs, they are valid because reasons can be given for them.

Crombie does not agree with views that suggest that religious truths are non-cognitive or symbolic, in the sense of theological and religious language being a mode of symbolic language being expressive in the moral or aesthetic sense - so he is opposed to the views of R.B. Braithwaite and J.H. Randall.

Nevertheless, Crombie appreciates that with regard to faith the issue of verification is problematic. Key issues have to do with what is consistent or compatible with the facts that support one's belief - and here the facts can be historical and experiential.

Crombie knows that some theologians try to avoid the **FAITH-FACTS** or **FAITH-HISTORY** interface, and philosophers like the logical positivists say that theological statements are meaningless anyway. He is also mindful of the distinction between "believing in" and "believing that". This is found in some of the debates over philosophy of religion in the 1950s in the wake of the later philosophy of Wittgenstein and has to do with the   contrast that can be drawn between factual beliefs ("belief that") and commitments and attitudes represented as "belief in".

Crombie takes a realist and correspondence view about truth; he argues that "belief that" is the presupposition for "belief in". (1957:32)

For example: you might **BELIEVE IN** Dr Smith's ability to get you through your Botany A level, but you have to believe that she exists for this "belief in" to be significant.

Crombie is strongly against the idea that religious language and faith can be reduced to an activity, a mode or form of life, or to the expression of feelings. Against this Crombie thinks there is for theological statements and the faith they express 'an irreducible element of belief' and he means that this has an objective character.

> "Christian faith and devotion is thought of by the Christian as an entry into relationship with a transcendent being, whom non-Christians do not believe to be there to enter into relationship with. Christian worship, therefore, is not only something which the non-Christian does not do, it is something which, by virtue of the difference of his beliefs, the non-Christian cannot do." (1957:32)

Crombie on "Theological Statements"

Crombie defends a classical view about religious language when he develops the idea that theological statements have a **PARADOXICAL CHARACTER**. He accepts that the critics of the claim that theological statements are meaningful base their view on the idea that such statements are paradoxical. They appear to be about something but they are not about anything that can be meaningfully verified. But Crombie comments:

> "These paradoxical features need not be regarded as demonstrating the impossibility of meaningful theological statements, but rather as contributing to a grasp of their meaning by giving a partial characterisation of their subject." (1957:34)

Crombie's aim is to argue that the term "God" is meaningful, yet mysterious and incomprehensible. The trick, if we put it that way, is to have a coherent explanation of how an incomprehensible mystery can yet be meaningful. This is what Crombie sets out to do.

Crombie suggests that the first step in theology is to understand that "God may not be identified with anything that can be indicated", this because the religious or faith aspect of the paradox in such statements results in the truth that such statements "are made about no object which falls within our normal experience, or any imaginable extension of our normal experience."

So, on Crombie's view theological statements are about a mystery, a mystery that can be elucidated via a consideration of the relationships between theological faith and the ethical commitments that have affinity with them - as in the 'Great Commandment' teaching in Mark 12, where the love of God is linked to loving my neighbour as myself. We are able to investigate the question as to whether a sense of mystery is appropriate to any part of our experience and by this means we can judge the sense of theological language.

Crombie thinks that the mystery aspect of theological language is a consequence of what, in faith terms and in the religious vocabulary within Christianity, we would term **REVELATION**, and this we can explain and express an understanding of, but we employ language paradoxically in this process - but we must keep clear the character of the paradox, which is summarised thus:

> *"The problem about theological statements is simply that there is a sense in which we cannot know what they are about (a sense in which we cannot know God) nor what it is that they assert." (1957:35)*

"Proper" and "improper" proper names

Crombie develops his idea of the paradoxical character of theological statements via the view that what goes on is a kind of "as if": when we make some statement of faith to express, in some sense, something of "God". We find a tension in that the statements:

> *"are to be interpreted as if their subject was a particular individual, and yet differ in logical character from all other statements about particular individuals." (1957:39)*

Crombie takes as an example the statement "Tom loves Mary." Assuming we know both Tom and Mary, if we are asked who Tom is, then we can point out who he is, and "Tom, the proper name, correlates to the individual in question. But if we say "The average man falls in love at least once between the ages of 18 and 27" and then ask "Who is the average man?", then the problem is that we are not showing that we understand the term **AVERAGE MAN**, (1957:48).

"Tom", says Crombie, operates as a proper proper name; it is directly about Tom. "The average man", to be clarified, needs to be reduced. It is **OBLIQUE** in its reference, and is about 'people in general'.

If we say "God loves mankind" the question "Who is God?" is proper and all the rules of grammar suggest a direct reference. But Crombie insists that "there is an improper sense in which it cannot be answered". Crombie then notes is that whilst in respect of "Who is Tom?" we have a procedure for introducing somebody to Tom, we have not such procedure for introducing somebody to God - unless, Crombie adds, "there are operations ... from the standpoint of faith",(1957:40).

Crombie makes clear in his discussion that the question of the meaningfulness of theological statements is a vital one for the sceptic: it is not an issue for a person of faith. But it comes to expression in the consequence of the review Crombie makes of the "Who is God?" question: the upshot is that this name ("God") is an **IMPROPER PROPER NAME** it isn't an oblique statement about a generality but also, it isn't about a being with whom one is acquainted in the way that we might be with Tom.

Crombie notes a number of other ways in which terms can be significant, although the rules of grammar get contradictory.

An illustration: the word "point"

POINT in geometry denotes that points are in space and that they are sizeless. Common sense and our usual rules of expression suggest that if something is "in space", it must have some size. A thought (of lunch, for example) can be sizeless, but it isn't usual to think of thoughts being in space like the London Eye or Clifton Suspension Bridge. Still, "point" operates in this "improper" manner in geometry.

Fictitious characters have proper names - Crombie takes "Titania" as his example. We can explain who Titania is relationally within the characters in A Midsummer Night's Dream but we can't literally point "Titania" out.

Crombie remarks that "the expression 'God' in some ways resembles words which stand for fictions."

Crombie does not want to press the comparisons with geometric points or fictions to illuminate theological statements - he uses the examples simply to show that we can, in a more modern phrase, "think outside the box" of usual grammatical expression when doing mathematics and drama - and we do this in theology too. This shows us that theological statements are in a "logically anomalous position":

> "On the one hand statements about God are not reducible, and in that they are like statements about Tom as opposed to statements about the average man. On the other hand, although they are not reducible, but have their own distinct subject, in the manner of 'Tom loves Mary', that subject is not an ordinary subject." (1957:41)

And:

> "*God is not known to anybody, and ... descriptions which are sometimes offered as uniquely characterising Him ('the first cause', 'the necessary being') are such that nobody can say what it would be like to conform to one of them (if one knew what it would be like for something to be a necessary being, then one could say that 'God' stood for whatever satisfies these conditions; but one does not.*" (1957:42-43)

Crombie argues that the character of statements about "God" are not distinct from other statements in purely logical or physical terms: this makes the question of the proper reference for the expression "God" hard to fix - and for Crombie this is where his argument turns: if we can identify an appropriate reference-range for an expression, then we can make sense of it.

Can we find a reference range for "God" and for theological statements?

Theological Statements: the problem of content and the issue of a reference-range of meaning

Crombie thinks that a further range of problems can be linked to theological statements if we ask more searchingly about their content, about what they are about. When theologians talk about God they reckon to express truths and to have definitions, albeit paradoxical ones, that express the sense of what they mean. However, the theologian will not allow that scientific enquiry can arbitrate the meaning of theological discourse. Phrases like "God loves us" can be used because the usual meanings of terms is clear to us and because in the faith context of expression, the phrase "acquires formal properties which render it utterly

119

baffling to the critic" (p. 48). Thus not only is the critic puzzled as to the reference of theological language, he is lost as to the nature of its content. The theist, however, is in the following state: "believing in a mystery beyond experience, traces of which he claims to detect in experience."

Thus Crombie suggests that the believer contends that:

> "He is obliged to use, for the expression of his beliefs, language governed by paradoxical rules." (1957:50)

Crombie then thinks that we can examine some affinities between theological and other statements to the end of helping to fix the reference range of theological language. This follows because the subject-matter of theological statements overlaps with the subject matter of empirical and moral statements. This means that "theological statements are sensitive to, and have affinities and relationships with statements of other kinds." (1957:51)

As examples of affinities and relationships Crombie notes ordinary language use, the language of psychology and related disciplines - as in theological statements about love, and moral language - in statements about the nature and extent of human suffering. Nevertheless, theological statements are in a real sense distinctive, irreducible, parabolic (see p. 70), and paradoxical and essentially this is because they are impelled by "a conception of the divine" (p. 54), that is to say, "a conception of a being outside time and space, on whom the spacio-temporal universe is in some sense dependent."

As consequence of this conception it follows that in theological discourse;

"It will not be possible, in any ordinary way, to indicate such a being, for indicating is selecting a region of space-time in which certain qualities are manifested." (1957:54-55)

Crombie argues:

"it also seems natural to suppose that if God is conceived as the source of the space-time universe, Himself outside space and time, His activity will not be manifested (at least normally) here rather than there (for then He would be here rather than there) and hence that statements about his relation to the created universe will not take the form of cosmological hypotheses, verifiable by observing the contents of particular spacio-temporal regions." (1957:55)

Crombie makes clear on a number of occasions the strict sense in which we can and can't speak meaningfully of God:

"We must acknowledge at once that in the ordinary sense we have no conception of the divine nature. We do not know God, and it would be absurd to claim that we know what sort of being He is." (1957:55)

Crombie's solution is as follows:

"What I propose to argue is could be put like this: the conception of the divine is indeed in one sense an empty notion; but it is the notion of a compliment which could fill in certain deficiencies in our experience, that could not be filled in by further experiences or scientific theory-making; and its positive

content is simply the idea of something (we know not what) which might supply those deficiencies." (1957:56)

Crombie favours the notion of GOD AS SPIRIT and he argues that within human life all kinds of things, such as love, feeling, hoping, are concepts needed for the description of human subjects that we don't need in the slightest when describing items in the natural world, like tables, computers or trees. Human subjects can of course be atomised physiologically, but there is nevertheless a distinction between the patient on the operating table as inspected by the surgeon, and the patient in herself, thinking, hoping, feeling, or praying. The dualism here is evident in the performance of an elective Caesarean or in some types of brain surgery when a general anaesthetic is not employed and the patient remain conscious throughout. Crombie is, in effect, arguing for a mode of duality in the nature of being human, in a tradition in philosophy from Aristotle to Gilbert Ryle. This is not an understanding that sees humans as body and soul in a sharply distinct manner, but it allows for humans to be described as spiritual beings, in the sense that "part of our experience of ourselves is only describable with the aid of concepts of a non-physical kind." (1957:58) This means that we make, consciously and deliberately, a category-error, in that we use a term for which we can give no proper meaning. Crombie makes it clear that whilst we can set out precise meanings for terms like "smile" or "digestion", we cannot do the same for "spirit".

> *"I admit that we have no idea of spirit, and claim only that it is extravagant to say that we have no notion whatsoever of how the word is used. How the word is used (and this, of course, defines such meaning as it has for us) in the theological context is by the deliberate commission of a category mistake under the pressure of convictions which require us to depart from normal*

language-practice in this way." (1957:60)

Crombie defines **GOD AS INFINITE SPIRIT**, and uses this to set out the reference-range for theological language in a negative sense, thus in an apophatic way. To employ the tern "infinite" is not to use the term in its mathematical sense: in respect of God,

> *"We mean, negatively that he is unlimited; or, more positively, that, being the source of all limitation, there is nothing whatsoever to which he is conformed, or to which He must conform Himself." (1957:62)*

"Infinite", like "necessary", "omnipotent", and "creator" are words used of "God", but the key characteristic, says Crombie, is that "in so far as they have any precise sense, they cannot be used about "God". For, since we do not know 'God', they cannot acquire a precise sense by reference to His properties; if then they have a precise sense they must acquire it from reference to the properties of something else; and since nothing else can be an adequate model for 'God', in so far as they have a precise sense, it cannot be applied to Him." (1957:62)

Here we see references to positive and negative theology recalling Dionysius, and a qualified use of analogy and models - so an overlap with Aquinas and I.T. Ramsey.

Crombie makes it clear that for the person of faith no issue arises over the language of theology or over the significance of "God": it refers to "a being who could claim one's adoration". Thus a case exists to fix the reference-range of theological language by looking, not at what is aid or felt about reality by religious people, but at "how they dispose themselves towards God - that is, to learn what worship is." Here Crombie in effect reactivates the via eminetiae we considered earlier.

Crombie continues:

> *"It is the contrast between the attitude of worship , and the attitude which religion commends towards creatures (always to be valued, but never, absolutely, in themselves) which illuminates what religion takes the infinite-finite contrast to be."*

Crombie notes that his work is the theoretical equivalent of the ban on idolatry in the Old Testament. His point is that the ban on idolatry "taught the Jews what God is."

Crombie (p. 64) considers the following pairs of terms:

- **FINITE - INFINITE**

- **CONTINGENT - NECESSARY**

- **DERIVATIVE - NON-DERIVATIVE**

As terms in theological language we should not seek to "anatomise" their meaning. If we say the world is "finite" we don't mean that "it can be counted or travelled across; when we speak of it as derivative, we do not think of it as derived from its origin by any normal kind of derivation."

The key thing is to see that in theology "the meaning to be attached to the second member of each pair is to be got at by seeing what kind of judgement about the world is intended by the use of the first." And the sort of judgment intended by such language is "an intellectual dissatisfaction with the notion that the universe is a complete system, with, as a corollary, the notion of a being with which one could be thus dissatisfied." (p. 65)

With the references to paradox so emphatically built into his theory, Crombie in a real sense returns us to the apophatic approach with which we began and Crombie's ideas can be criticised in much the same way as the apophatic tradition, just as his present a challenge to reductionist critics.

KEY TERMS

Meaningful Tautology - Faith and Discernment (the penny drops) - Models and Qualifiers - 'belief that' and 'belief in' - Paradox - Proper and Improper Names - Logical Anomaly - Reference Range (for religious/theological language)

FURTHER READING

Ferré (1970) gives the themes considered here very secure treatment. Crombie's article is in Mitchell (1957) and Santoni (1968). Ramsey (1957) is a classic text.

SELF-ASSESSMENT QUESTIONS

1. Illustrate and explain how Ramsey gives empirical placement to theological/religious language.

2. Illustrate and explain Ramsey's ideas on faith and discernment.

3. Make detailed notes on Ramsey's ideas of "models and qualifiers".

4. Research and collate ideas for a critical review of Ramsey especially in relation to the challenge of verificationism.

5. Make notes on the ways in which Crombie uses the idea of paradox.

6. Illustrate and explain Crombie's argument about "proper" and "improper proper" names.

7. Make notes so the idea of a reference-range for meaning can be explained and reviewed.

8. 8. Illustrate Crombie's use of what might be called a version of the "via eminentiae".

And two A2-style questions:

9. Critically assess the view that religious language has meaning because it has empirical placement.

10. To what extent is paradoxical language about God meaningful?

Conclusion

Throughout this topic there has been tension between two basic standpoints. Firstly, the view that all truth-claims must be bound in propositional statements, and then be subjected to the checks of verifiability or falsification. Secondly, the view that there are legitimate truths which, by their nature, can be expressed in ways that are representational and coherent, but not literal or factual. Thus, looking over the material we have reviewed there are clear differences that we find in the attempts to operate with a definitive criterion of meaning and truth for all language; the principle of verification, the principle of falsification, the picture-theory of meaning of the early Wittgenstein, for example; all variations on a theme, perhaps.

In contrast, the variety of characterisations given to religious language, including views which suggest that humans operate in textured, are layered and multi-dimensional worlds of discourse. Tillich with his notion of realms and levels of meaning and the later Wittgenstein's ideas of language games and forms of life offer such perspectives - variations on another theme.

The paradoxical unsayability of what religious language nevertheless tries to say has been a constant theme in the ideas we have considered. This is found in the apophatic tensions between positive and negative theology, over the use of analogy and the importance of seeing symbolic language aright, and in Crombie's reasoning about theological language as considered above.

It perhaps worth closing with a brief reflection on this via three strands of thought, two of which we have already encountered.

Kant writes that his object in Critique of Pure Reason (1781) was that of "denying knowledge in order to make room for faith" (1929:29). He argues this because he thinks that "Human reason has this peculiar fate that in one species of its knowledge it is burdened by questions which, as prescribed by the very nature of reason itself, it is not able to ignore, but which, as transcending all its powers, it is also not able to answer", (p. 7). He means that there are genuine "ultimate questions" which we cannot ignore, but neither can we can answer them. Thus we cannot have knowledge, but we can live and act in faith.

Wittgenstein says in the Tractatus (1921) that:

> "There are, indeed, things that cannot be put into words. They make themselves manifest. They are what is mystical." (6.522)

He too affirms action rather than theory as the right response.

Finally the poet T.S. Eliot (1888-1965) writes in his Four Quartets (1935-1942) in a manner charged with apophatic intent, with the mystic St John of the Cross very much in mind. Writing of love, commitment, and of devotion to that which is of deepest value, he comments on the "intolerable wrestle/With words and meanings" (2001:15), and on how:

> "Words strain,/Crack and sometimes break, under the burden,/ Under the tension, slip, slide, perish,/Decay with imprecision, will not stay in place,/ Will not stay still." (2001:8)

He has the apophatic line "I said to my soul, be still, and let the dark come upon you/ Which shall be the darkness of God", (p. 16).

And this passage of paradoxical reflection:

"In order to arrive there,
To arrive where you are, to get from where you are not, You
must go by a way wherein there is no ecstasy.
In order to arrive at what you do not know

You must go by a way which is the way of ignorance. In order to
possess what you do not possess
You must go by the way of dispossession.
In order to arrive at what you are not

You must go through the way in which you are not. And what
you do not know is the only thing you know And what you own
is what you do not own
And where you are is where you are not." (2001:17-18)

We have seen views offering variations of clarity and risks of reductionism; and other arguments offering degrees of relativism but risks of ambiguity and a loss of perspective. A central idea emerging is that poetic, philosophical and theological language all makes a particular use of paradoxical language. As we saw in the first chapter, some scholars point out that paradox can be argued to be indistinguishable from contradiction; others argue that in relation to certain modes of insight paradoxical expression is truly fitting. In this debate the problem of religious language has its centre and the focus for ongoing study.

Bibliography

- **ANSELM** - (1973) The Prayers and Meditations of Saint Anselm, Translated and Introduced by Benedicata Ward, Penguin, Harmondsworth.

- **AYER, A.J.** - (1970) Language Truth and Logic, London, Gollancz.

- **AQUINAS** - Summa Theologica.

- **AQUINAS** - (1998) Selected Writings. Edited and translated by R. McInerny, Penguin, London.

- **BULTMANN, R.** - (1958) Jesus Christ and Mythology, Scribners, NY.

- **CHARLESWORTH, M.** - (2002) Philosophy and Religion, Oneworld, Oxford.

- **CROMBIE, I.** - "The Possibility of Theological Statements" in Mitchell (1957) pp. 31-83.

- **DAVIES, B.** - (1986) An Introduction to the Philosophy of Religion, OUP, Oxford.

- **PSEUDO-DIONYSUS** - The Aeropagite (1980) The Divine Name and Mystical Theology, Translated by J. Jones, MUP, Milwauke

- **ELIOT T.S.** - (2001) Four Quartets, Faber, London.

- **FERRE, F.** - (1970) Language, Logic and God, Fontana, London.

- **FLEW, A.** - (2008) There is a God, HarperOne, NY.

- **FLEW, A. & MACINTYRE, A.** - (1955) New Essays in Philosophical Theology, SCM, London.

- **GENOVA, J.** - (1995) Wittgenstein A Way of Seeing. Routledge, London.

- **HICK, J.** - (1974) Faith and Knowledge, Fontana, London.

- **HICK, J.** - (1990) The Philosophy of Religion, (4th edition) Prentice Hall, NJ.

- **KANT, I.** - (1929) Critique of Pure Reason, (Kemp Smith edition), Macmillan, London.

- **MAGEE, B.** - (1975) Popper, Fontana/Collins, Glasgow.

- **MAGEE, B.** - (ed) (1986) Modern British Philosophy, OUP, Oxford.

- **MAIMONIDES, M.** - (1904) A Guide for the Perplexed, translated from the original Arabic text by M.

- **FRIEDLAENDER** - 4th revised ed. New York: E.P. Dutton.

- **MITCHELL, B.** - (ed) (1957) Faith and Logic, Allen and Unwin, London.

- **POPPER, K.** - (1981) Conjectures and Refutations, RKP, London.

- **MACQUARRIE, J.** - (1966) Principles of Christian Theology, SCM, London.

- **PLANTIGNA, A.** - "Religious Belief as 'Properly Basic'" in C. Taliaferro and P. Griffiths, eds, (2003) pp 200- 225

- **PHILLIPS, D.Z.** - (1971) Death and Immortality, London, Macmillan.

- **PHILLIPS, D.Z.** - (1999) Philosophy's Cool Place, Ithaca: Cornell University Press.

- **ROBINSON, J.M.** - (2007) Jesus According the Earliest Witness, Fortress Press, Minneapolis.

- **SANTONI, R.** - (ed) (1968) Religious Language and the Problem of Religious Knowledge, Indiana University Press, Bloomington.

- **SMART, N.** - (1969) The Religious Experience of Mankind, Fontana, London.

- **SMART, N.** - (1970) Philosophy of Religion, Sheldon Press, London.

- **SMART, N.** - (1998) Dimensions of the Sacred: An Anatomy of the World's Beliefs, UCA Press.

- **TALIAFERRO, C.** & **GRIFFITHS, P.** - (eds) (2003) Philosophy of Religion An Anthology, Blackwell, Oxford.

- **TILLICH**, P. - (1968) Systematic Theology, Nisbet (Single Volume edition), London. (2009) Dynamics of Faith, HarperOne, NY

- **WAINWRIGHT, W.** - (ed) (2005) The Oxford Handbook of Philosophy of Religion, OUP, Oxford.

- **WARD, K.** - (2008) Re-thinking Christianity, Oneworld, Oxford.

- **WILLIAMS, B.** - (1955) 'Turtullian's Paradox', in Flew & MacIntyre (1955)

- **WISFOM, J.** - (1953) 'Philosophical Perplexity', in Philosophy & Psychoanalysis, Oxford

- **WITTGENSTEIN, L.** - (1953) Philosophical Investigations, (Anscombe edn) Blackwell, Oxford.

- **WITTGENSTEIN, L.** - (1961) Tractatus Logico-Philosophicus, (Pears and McGuiness edn) RKP, London.

- **WITTGENSTEIN, L.** - (1980) Culture and Value, (Von Wright/ Winch edn) UCP, Chicago.

- **WITTGENSTEIN, L.** - (1993) Philosophical Occasions (ed. Klagge and Nordham), Hackett, Indianapolis.

Postscript

Stephen Loxton is a graduate of the Universities of Sussex and Hull and is Head of Religious Studies and Philosophy at Sherborne School for Girls, where he is also Theory of Knowledge Coordinator for the International Baccalaureate. He teaches AS Philosophy of Religion and Ethics and A2 New Testament and Ethics as well as Philosophy within the I.B. programme. He holds advanced degrees in Philosophy and Theology as well as an M.Phil from Hull University.

Stephen would like to dedicate this book to Marie Fenn.

Students seeking fuller explanations and a bibliography should also consult the website which also contains exam tips and past questions listed by theme.